Recommender Systems for Information Providers

Andreas W. Neumann

Recommender Systems
for Information Providers

Designing Customer Centric
Paths to Information

Physica-Verlag

A Springer Company

Dr. Andreas W. Neumann
Universität Karlsruhe (TH)
Institute of Information Systems and Management
School of Economics and Business Engineering
Kaiserstraße 12
76128 Karlsruhe
Germany
a.neumann@iism.uni-karlsruhe.de

ISBN 978-3-7908-2133-8   e-ISBN 978-3-7908-2134-5

DOI 10.1007/978-3-7908-2134-5

Contributions to Management Science ISSN 1431-1941

Library of Congress Control Number: 2009920043

Cover design: Integra Software Services Pvt. Ltd., Puducherry

Printed on acid-free paper

9 8 7 6 5 4 3 2 1

springer.com

Preface

Recommender systems have recently been integrated into several Internet stores. Generally, a recommender system reads observed customer behavior or opinions from customers as input, then aggregates and directs the resulting recommendations to appropriate recipients. Customers profit from a faster finding of relevant products; stores profit from rising sales. Information providers, e. g. the various players in the publishing industry, are a very promising application area of recommender systems due to high search costs for their goods and the general problem of assessing the quality of information products. Nevertheless, the usage of recommendation services in this market is still very sparse. The goal of this book is to present all aspects of recommender systems as customer centric paths to information products in online platforms from a practical point of view.

Consequentially, this book is targeted not only towards researchers but practitioners as well. It describes all steps it takes to design, implement, and successfully operate a recommender system for a specific information platform. All scientific results and developed methods presented within this book are proven in real-world applications open to the general public. Data and experiences from these applications are given as case studies. In summary, this book describes all aspects of recommender systems: the economic background, mechanism design, a survey of existing systems in the WWW, statistical methods and algorithms, service oriented architectures for implementation, user interfaces, as well as experiences from and analyses of real-world applications. After reading this book, practitioners should be able to decide whether and how they might want to integrate recommender systems into their applications.

This text is not intended as a classroom textbook. It does not give detailed introductions for students on all possible recommendation generating algorithms. In a very subjective manner, it focuses on solutions to those problems, that I found to be most critical—and least answered by the existing literature—while developing several recommender systems for different information providers in the last years.

Researchers will be able to find new techniques that are not yet widely published but have already proven their applicability in several Internet applications. This includes anonymous behavior-based recommender systems for areas with strong privacy concerns or not-logged-in users, scalable algorithms especially suited for large collections of products (e. g. library catalogs with more than 10,000,000 documents), as well as solutions to lessen the cold start problem of behavior-based systems. Wherever alternative methods exist, they are briefly discussed. For more details, references to the original publications are provided throughout the book.

The case studies and the included statistical data are mainly focused on scientific and technical information providers, especially libraries. Within this market, many live tests with real users were possible, that would not have been approved by executives of most e-commerce companies. In this context, I would like to thank the University Library of Karlsruhe for letting me conduct large field experiments to test various theories and algorithms using their main website. Further on, my special thanks go to its many anonymous users who contributed to the installed recommender systems without being aware of the research going on in the background. Though conducted with library users, the economic analyses presented show why the results obtained from these studies are also applicable in a much more general e-commerce environment.

I gratefully acknowledge the support of the German Research Foundation (DFG). Some of the results presented in this book were developed while I was working on various DFG funded projects at the Institute of Information Systems and Management at the Universität Karlsruhe (TH).

Karlsruhe, November 2008   *Dr. Andreas W. Neumann*

Contents

1

Introduction

Various online stores have recently integrated different kinds of recommender systems in their e-commerce storefronts. Thereby, the general public is becoming more and more accustomed and positively attached to these value-adding services. Recommender systems in online stores present products as recommendations to customers according to the customers' current interests and needs. On the one hand, customers profit from a faster finding of relevant products, on the other hand, stores profit from rising sales.

Scientific and technical information providers, e.g. university libraries, are a very promising application area of recommender systems as well. Nevertheless, the usage of recommendation services in this market is still in its infancy. The goal of this book is to present economical concepts, statistical methods and algorithms, technical architectures, as well as experiences from case studies on how recommender systems can be integrated at providers of scientific and technical information.

1.1 Recommender Systems

In everyday life we have to make choices in areas of little or no personal experience. A common solution to this problem lies in asking peers. Recommendation letters for job applications, movie reviews in newspapers, or restaurant guides are a first step of scaling-up the social word of mouth process. Recommender systems aggregate knowledge from many peer groups to the level of expert advice services. They better the social process and bear the potential to significantly reduce transaction costs for the consumer by means of their aggregation capabilities.

Generally speaking, a recommender system reads observed user behavior or opinions from users as input, then aggregates and directs the resulting recommendations to appropriate recipients. The developers of the first recommender system—Tapestry developed at the Xerox Palo Alto Research Center [GNOT92]—introduced the term "collaborative filtering", which was later adopted by several others. "Recommender system" was coined by Resnick and Varian in 1997 [RV97] to better describe the action than "collaborative filtering" for two reasons: first, recommenders may not explicitly collaborate with recipients, who may be unknown to each other, and second, recommendations may suggest particularly interesting items, in addition to indicating those that should be filtered out. On the one hand, recommender systems bear the potential to significantly reduce the transaction costs of finding a suitable product for a specific customer need. On the other hand, recommender systems can be utilized as community tools featuring the interaction of customers. This helps to intensify the relationship with customers in the long run. When focusing on the information channel aspect of recommender systems, the term "recommendation service" is used. Recommendation services are market information systems of electronic markets. A recommender system might manage a bundle of different recommendation services.

Recommender systems, especially when based on the approach of explicitly asking the users for input, are built upon the vision of the "prosumer"—sometimes also used in the form "prosumption". The portmanteau prosumer stems from merging producer and consumer. This idea was first described—although not named—by Toffler in his 1970's book "Future Shock" [Tof70]. In a market saturated by mass production of standardized products, businesses are forced to a process of mass customization for growing profit. For such a high degree of customization the participation of customers in the production process is necessary. Pine [PI93] describes the shift from mass production to mass customization as well as the necessary organizational changes for this new business competition. The rise of e-commerce has not so much influenced the production variety of physical goods, but made possible the customization of services and even of the shops themselves. Concerning services, in classical organizations the idea of the prosumer was pursued through various self-service approaches (restaurants, automatic teller machines, etc.), in e-organizations the idea can be pursued even more consequently by supplying electronic tools to the customers. Recommender systems are one important building block for a high level of personalization in e-commerce. Presenting every customer his personal shop with tailored services is a way to introduce the idea of mass customization to e-commerce. Recommender systems support a customization of the consumer experience in the presentation of the products sold at an online shop. By means of this, a different store personally designed for each customer becomes possible. By means of his explicit input together with his behavior each prosumer creates his own store.

Today's participants of online communities like Flickr[1] or YouTube[2], the so-called Web 2.0, are prototypes of prosumers. Amazon.com[3] with its recommender services is sometimes considered to books what is Flickr to photos or YouTube to videos. It serves as a platform for consumers to discuss about books by means of the review and rating recommendation services. Every user of a well designed recommender system not only consumes information but produces recommendations as well.

Recommender systems are related to marketing systems but taking a somehow reversed approach. Classical marketing systems help the marketer by grouping consumers and products and then match the resulting marketing segments and product categories for campaign management. Recommender systems start with direct interaction with consumers to guide them to products according to their needs and interests. Another relative of recommender systems can be found in supply-chain decision-support systems. To decide about the quantity of production and the distribution to warehouses and stores, these systems give predictions about aggregated consumption of segments of customers, e. g. the predicted demand in a specific city within a certain month. Recommender systems deal with the same sort of questions on the level of individual consumers. Recommendations are products that the system predicts this specific consumer in this moment to buy with a much higher than average probability. Summing up, by gathering data and guiding the customers to the right products, recommender systems can reduce the general marketing costs for the shop or service provider.

Recommender systems support sales at online stores in at least three ways [SKR01]:

Turning visitors into buyers. The majority of visitors browsing an online store leave without a purchase. Recommender systems help, by pointing to suitable products, to turn those visitors into buyers, who would have left the store because they didn't find a suitable product although it was somewhere in the store.

---

[1] http://flickr.com
[2] http://www.youtube.com
[3] http://www.amazon.com

Increasing cross-sell. Recommending additional items associated with the products in the shopping cart before the checkout process brings the customer back to the shelves and thereby can significantly increase cross-sell.

Locking-in the customers. In the Internet the competitor is always just one click away; gaining consumer loyalty is an essential business strategy. From the supplier's perspective an installed base of customers should be locked-in. The extent of a customer's lock-in is measured by the switching costs to a competitor. The more a customer uses the recommender systems—teaching it about his interests and needs—the more he becomes locked-in to the supplier. "Even if a competitor were to build the exact same capabilities, a customer ... would have to spend an inordinate amount of time and energy teaching the competitor what the company already knows" [PIPR95]. Considering behavior-based recommender systems that analyze the purchase history of a customer, this data might even be completely lost when switching to a competitor.

1.2 Scientific and Technical Information

Recommender systems are valuable tools in many areas. This book puts a special emphasis on the market of STI. Although recommender systems are especially valuable in information economics, they still hardly exist for scientific information.

In this work, the term STI is used very broadly. It includes every information that is of value to the academic community or the research and development department of any organization. It is considered as a synonym to "information of STM" (science, technology, and medicine), which can sometimes be found in the literature as well. Most of today's STI exists in the form of journal articles or books. Other media types that play a growing role include but are not limited to CDs, DVDs, audio and video files, interactive computer graphics or programs, and collections of raw statistical data from experiments and surveys. The more of these media types an information research tool supports, the more helpful it generally is to the users.

Information goods as a key resource of the 21st century might even displace industrial goods as key drivers of markets. Not only is the foundation of the developed countries' economic prosperity based on the efficient conversion of information to knowledge, but also on distributing this knowledge in the educational system. In this context, providers of scientific and technical information play a decisive role for the economic wealth of a society. Valid and credible information is a scarce resource. Information consumes the attention of its recipients. "Hence a wealth of information creates a poverty of attention and a need to allocate that attention efficiently among the overabundance of information sources that might consume it" [Sim71]. Recommender systems are tools in the economics of attention, they help to filter out the noise.

Although some particularities of STI exist, the general market for STI should be evaluated by means of the same attributes as other industries: price, quality, and entry. A large number of studies exist about the market of STI due to the attention of public decision makers (see Section 2.1). On the one hand, this attention stems from the fact that science has a key role in fostering economic growth. On the other hand, the funding structure of goods of STI is unique: a large part of the scientific activity is publicly funded, the output is typically "donated" to privately owned journals, so is the majority of refereeing services, and finally, these journals are bought by publicly-funded libraries. This structure is in question by many public authorities because of its seemingly lacking relative efficiency. One of the many problems within this market is the fact that libraries have only an imperfect knowledge of the value of the journals for the end users. Facilitating aggregated data from recommender systems for collection management purposes helps libraries to decide, which journals are essential for their customer group of scientists.

The cost structure of an information supplier differs from other industries. The production of information in general is costly but the reproduction is cheap. Even in the non-digital world, books that cost hundreds of thousands of Euros to produce can be printed and bound for a few Euros. Intellectual property rights to restrict the reproduction helps to ensure the production of information. But a too conservative approach of the management of intellectual property can also hinder the development of new revenue sources [SV99]. Information goods have high fixed costs but low marginal costs. One of the implications of this is that cost-based pricing doesn't work, the goods must be priced according to consumer value. A field experiment on the pricing of digital scientific information conducted by the author showed that even for very low prices below 1.00 Euro a significant price elasticity of demand exists, allowing for pricing based on consumer value [Neu07c, Neu07b]. Recommender systems can help to determine the specific value of a good to a customer allowing for a detailed level of differential pricing.

STI is an experience good: consumers must experience every new article or book to value it. It is impossible to determine the value of the good before the transaction, or, as Arrow puts it in his classical paper [Arr62]: "... there is a fundamental paradox in the determination of demand for information; its value for the purchaser is not known until he has the information, but then he has in effect acquired it without cost." The market of STI is a market with asymmetric information, which occurs when the seller knows more about a product than the buyer. Akerlof, Spence, and Stiglitz have made early and significant contributions to the analysis of markets of this kind (see e. g. [Ake70, Spe74, RS76]). Branding and reputation, e. g. of the authors or the publisher, are a way to value STI before the consumption. But recommender systems can help to value a specific information good for an individual customer before the purchase. The characteristic of STI as experience goods makes recommender systems especially useful in STI markets.

A particularity of the market of STI is the large number of different available products. A large library contains tens of millions of documents exceeding by far the number of any large consumer store. This leads to higher search costs for information goods; search costs have been an early area of concern in the economics of information (see e. g. [Sti61]). Further on, the evaluation of the quality of a scientific document is very hard and time consuming even if the content is already available. In new research fields acknowledged experts that could be referenced might not even yet exist. This makes automatic research tools that estimate the quality of the information exceptionally helpful.

This work will not go into detail, in which format the STI reaches the customer. Technology has just the meaning of the packaging of the information by which it reaches the end consumer. Sometimes Internet technology is portrayed as a threat to the information business for its copying and sharing capabilities. But it should be stated, that "the technology infrastructure makes information more accessible and hence more valuable" [SV99]. More customers can be reached and the delivering of the information good was never as easy as it is today. It is a matter of the business concept to use this opportunity. The changes this brings to the market of STI are discussed in the Chapter 2.

1.3 Motivation and Focus

Although recommendation services are frequent in e-commerce storefronts, they hardly exist at STI providers. Scientific libraries, the most widespread form of providers of STI, have been somehow slow to integrate recommender services in their online public access catalogs (OPAC). At libraries the profit contribution of a product (library document) is not the first concern and the customers (library users) are coming due to very different incentives compared to online stores of physical consumer goods. Nevertheless, libraries are still definitively a very promising application area. Due to the supply complexity or the cost of evaluation of the quality, technicians, scientists, and students are more and more incapable of efficiently finding relevant literature in conventional database oriented catalog systems and search engines. A common solution to this problem lies in asking peers for recommendations of reading's on the topic of interest. Recommender systems aggregate knowledge from many peer groups to the level of expert advice services, thus optimizing the approach taken before by many single individuals separately. By means of recommendation services library OPACs can be turned into customer oriented service portals supporting the interaction of the customers.

The approach of stakeholders, i. e. system managers and users, towards recommender systems depends on the application area. Although algorithms to compute recommendations might often be applicable in many areas, when it comes to motivation and incentives of stakeholders, different mechanisms are at work in different application areas. The mechanism design of a recommender service is a very critical aspect when it comes to the long term success of the service. Therefore, a profound analysis of the market of scientific information is necessary to successfully integrate recommender systems at providers of STI.

Considering technical aspects, the typical legacy information architectures differ widely from one area to the other. E-commerce shopping applications are built from other basic modules than library OPAC software. Last but not least, the number of products in (compound) library catalogs are often counted in tens or hundreds of millions, exceeding by far the number of products of any consumer store. This leads to new types of scalability problems that do not exist in most e-commerce applications. Suitable statistical algorithms for periodic incremental updates of the computed recommendations have to go hand in hand with scalable database and service architectures.

The motivation of this work lies in developing the necessary components to make possible the successful integration of recommender systems at providers of STI. When it comes to the market of STI, the focus is set on scientific libraries. The developed systems have been integrated as standard services open to the general public into the

OPACs of different libraries. Thereby, firsthand experience and evaluations of the new developed scientific techniques could be gained and are presented in the next chapters as well.

1.4 Chapter Guide

This book is structured in the following way. Chapter 2 gives an introduction to the market of STI. The players in the market are analyzed by means of a special value-chain presentation. It is shown that the strategic disposition of value-adding search and community tools like recommender systems is crucial to the future success of the players to intensify their relationship to repeat customers. Chapter 3 starts with a classification of recommender systems before analyzing the pros and cons of different systems. Designing recommender systems means designing games of static mechanism design, a special class of games of incomplete information. The different classes of recommender systems are evaluated in a qualitative way by their mechanism design problems and solutions. A survey of existing recommender systems at major STI providers is given in Chapter 4. Although some scientific digital libraries are experimenting with such systems, they are generally still no standard features. Next, in Chapter 5 the focus is set on explicit recommender systems. The integration of group-specific rating and review services into the OPAC of the University Library of Karlsruhe is described as a case study. Usage statistics are given and the services are evaluated. Chapters 6 to 8 study behavior-based systems in more detail. Chapter 6 gives an overview of the general concepts of behavior-based recommendations, as there are preference theory, self-selection, data-mining, and diffusion processes. In Chapter 7 different algorithms to compute recommendations from behavioral data are described. The application of these algorithms is shown in Chapter 8. There, detailed integration information of behavior-based services in different university libraries as well as national and international compound catalogs can be found. In Chapter 9 a new interface for the visualization and exploration of information spaces is presented and evaluated. Finally, Chapter 10 gives an overall discussion of the main results of this study.

2

The Market of Scientific and Technical Information

In Chapter 1 it was argued that STI plays a decisive role for the long term economic wealth of a population. The main players involved in the production of STI are authors, scientific libraries, publishers, bookstores, scientific associations, and collecting societies. This chapter examines the role of the different players in the market to determine where the introduction of recommender systems is a strategic option to gain further impact on the market in the future. In order to do this, a structural model for the value chain of the production within STI markets is developed based on the 2-3-6-concept, a special value chain presentation. The analysis reveals that none of the players can be expected to stay within its historically grown core competencies. Due to technical developments—generally summarized as the process of digitization—and the associated changes concerning the structure of transaction costs, each player can cover more fields of value adding activities. Setting a stronger focus on portal and search services like recommender systems is a strategic positioning recommendation for scientific libraries, publishers, bookstores, and scientific associations (with different priorities) in order to persist in the STI market of the future.

2.1 Information Providers in the Digital Age

The very heart of the business of information providers lies in collecting documents and delivering this information. Since information and communication are highly influential elements of our society, many public funded scientific libraries with long traditions exist to secure the collected knowledge of humankind. Changes of the worldwide educational systems within the last decades have lead to a growing production and demand of STI; more people than ever before are working in the scientific community. Digitization offers the technical means that enable information providers to cope with the growing data storage and transfer volumes. The process of digitization has conquered different classical segments of the STI market at different speeds. Reasons for the delayed adoption of the technology of the digital age and its possibilities are manifold. They include—but are not limited to—legal and contractual aspects like intellectual property rights with the technical issue of digital rights management as well as economical aspects like missing standardization in the industry or failures of the market. Scientific journals e. g. are already mostly available in digital form, while most books are still exclusively sold as paper copies. In some contexts the term digital interactive services (DIS) is used. DIS stands for the industry which has evolved around the electronic commerce for digital information goods. The core science, technology, and medicine publishing market is estimated between U. S. Dollar 7,000,000,000 and U. S. Dollar 11,000,000,000, while in 2001 OECD countries (members of the Organization for Economic Co-operation and Development) allocated U. S. Dollar 638,000,000,000 to research and development [DGL+06].

Lifelong learning as well as the growing sector of e-learning increase the demand of STI even further [Dea97]. Especially in the e-learning context, digital STI services are necessary to prevent discontinuities in the used media (e. g. switching back to paper) [KGKF01]. General or issue-related document delivery services are playing an important role in supplying individuals with STI when institutional flat rates are not available. Besides the market of the academic sector, a multitude of commercial service providers are offering digital STI.[1] For example, the service subito[2] of research libraries in Germany, Austria, and Switzerland has grown from 101,756 orders in 1998 to 1,339,902 in 2005. 84.5% of the deliveries in 2005 were ordered by non-commercial customers with a great share from academic institutions and 15.5% of the orders came from commercial customers from various industries paying higher prices. The subito history is accompanied by legal disputes with publishing companies trying to shut it down. In the year 2006 the deliveries dropped the first time back to a total of 1,225,323 due to a service stop in certain countries for legal reasons. [NHS02] presents a more detailed analysis of this service. Further information on the issue of pricing of digital information with a focus on document delivery services can be found in [Neu07c]. The politically planned change of the rights of creators of copyrighted works in Germany (Urheberrecht) in

---

[1] http://www.sub.uni-goettingen.de/ebene_1/1_doklie.htm
[2] http://www.subito-doc.de

the year 2008 will bring more changes to these type of services and the whole STI industry and market.

Although new players could enter the market trying to overtake the traditional players by consequently facilitating all technical means of the digital age, this hardly ever happens. It can be observed that all players in the market of STI are taking part in the process of digitization step by step. For example, setting up new purely digital libraries rarely occurs. Usually the traditional paper-oriented scientific libraries are extended to handle digital documents and are turned into so-called hybrid libraries, which then not only contain paper documents, but digital content as well. A few successful counterexamples can be found in the area of public authority funded digital archives like PubMed Central[3]. PubMed Central is the U.S. American National Institutes of Health free digital archive of biomedical and life science journal literature. In most cases the driving factor behind setting up completely new services is the public authorities' dissatisfaction with the pricing policy of quasi monopolistic publishers, in case of PubMed Central with the publisher Elsevier. It is often questioned if today's scientific journals still fulfill their double role of certification and dissemination in an optimal way. The main issue for the public authorities is the fact that in the process of publication the copyright of the majority of scientific results of publicly funded research is transferred to private publishing companies. The public authorities (who already financed the original research in the first place) then have to pay a second time to make the results accessible to other researchers. The subscription prices of scientific journals have been steadily increasing in the last 30 years. Between 1975 and 1995, they increased 200%–300% beyond inflation and were accompanied by a fall in subscriptions both by individual researchers and by scientific libraries. Journal prices far outpaced the evolution of library budgets, which did increase at a somewhat slower pace than total academic research budgets [DGL+06]. The first digital access models were introduced by publishers in 1995. Although this dramatically simplified the technical access for research, actual access still relies on the payment of subscriptions. A lot of studies are taking place trying to solve the question how the future of the market of STI should look like [Art01, Deu01, Kie01, DGL+06]. The open accessibility for the scientific community or for the taxpayers to the scientific results they produced or financed, respectively, is the most common goal for the public authorities. [OMS05] presents the results of a survey about the usage of open access publishers among scientists, a study

---

[3] http://www.pubmedcentral.nih.gov

of the financial and non-financial effects of alternative business models for scholarly journals can be found in [Kau05].

Most of the problems of the technical realization of STI processes have already been solved due to early research activities. These results have already helped with the integration at many information providers. Therefore, the focus here is not set on technical details. References to the early technical issues can be found e. g. within projects such as the "Stanford Digital Library Project"[4] within the U. S. American "Digital Library Initiative Phase 2"[5] or the Chablis-Project [BKEJ+98] within the program "Distributed Processing and Delivery of Digital Documents" (Schwerpunktprogramm Verteilte Vermittlung und Verarbeitung Digitaler Dokumente – V^3D^2) of the German Research Foundation (DFG)[6]. When it comes to the question, how recommender systems can be integrated into the developed STI library and service platforms, more information and case studies will be presented in the later chapters.

The main concern of this chapter is to identify players that will profit from the introduction of recommendation services and to determine what kind of role these systems can play in the strategic position of the players in the market. The relevant players in the market are: authors, bookstores, collecting societies, consumers, copy equipment manufacturers and operators, public authorities, publishers, scientific associations, and scientific libraries. Before the activities of the main players are analyzed in detail, the interaction of the players in the market is portrayed.

Figure 2.1 depicts the traditional flow of physical goods, information and money between the players. For reasons of clarity, only the flows of the most common classical business models of the market are shown. For example, depending on the market power of the journal, sometimes authors have to pay for their article to be published even if they also have to transfer the copyright to the publisher and the journal is not open access. Since this is not the general approach, no monetary flow from the author to the publisher is plotted. Further on, one has to keep in mind that the same person can take multiple roles within the market of STI. For example, most authors of scientific publications are consumers of STI as well. The process of digitization will change—and as a matter of fact with some participants already has—the interaction schemes shown. This includes the merging of players as well. Depending

---

[4] http://www-diglib.stanford.edu
[5] http://www.dli2.nsf.gov
[6] http://www.dfg.de

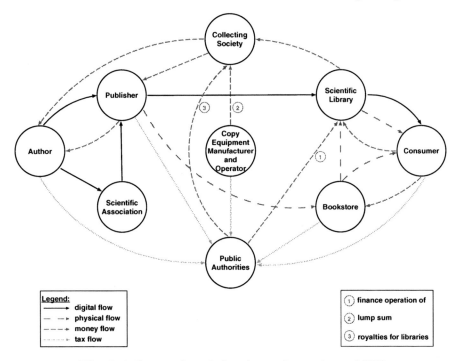

Fig. 2.1. Interaction of the players in markets of STI

on the viewpoint, the foundation of publishing houses within scientific associations can either be seen as a merger of the roles of the two players into a new kind of player, or as one legal person taking on different roles at the same time. Figure 2.1 portrays the traditional role of a scientific association focusing on scientific content and its creation outside of profit-oriented publishing activities. How this is changing—or already has—will be discussed in Section 2.3.5.

Copy equipment manufacturers and operators, public authorities, and collecting societies are in no position now or after changes in the market through the process of digitization to offer recommendation services to customers, therefore their activities will not be analyzed in detail in this chapter. Collecting societies (in Germany e. g. the Verwertungsgesellschaft Wort[7]) provide an indirect payment service and can not be seen as normal players within the value chain. Therefore they are, unfortunately, not included in several studies [Art01, Kie01] and not explicitly taken into account, although they influence the structure of STI markets with the transaction cost they impose on market par-

---

[7] http://www.vgwort.de

ticipants. The possible reproduction of information via copying adds
some special features to the market of STI. Collecting societies were
installed to solve the problem of fair distribution of the value-added. In
Figure 2.1 their role can be seen as an agent taking money from different players and redistributing it towards those players not able to get
a fair remuneration otherwise. Digital rights management might lead
to a more exact method of this distribution process away from lump
sums. Several service providers offer payment services which can be easily integrated into digital processes [KS02]. A more detailed economic
analysis of the market of STI can be found in [GSNHS03].

2.2 The 2-3-6-Value-Chain for STI Markets

In this section a structural model for the value chain of the market of
STI is developed based on [NHS02] and [GSNHS03]. The systematic
analysis of the development options of market participants made possible by technological progress helps to identify the application area and
potential of recommender systems for scientific and technical information providers. To understand the roles of the players in the market the
so called 2-3-6 concept [EA96] for DIS is applied. Schlueter and Shaw
[SS97] analyze DIS structures and dynamics in the area of e-commerce
by means of the 2-3-6-concept. In this book, the 2-3-6-concept is used
to identify the market potential of recommender systems at the players
in the STI market. Starting with the assignment of relevant activities
of core processes to the players a qualitative analysis of the dynamic
changes in the strategic positions of the players becomes possible.

The 2-3-6-value-chain first separates two horizontal strings of processes: one string for the scientific and technical content and one infrastructure string (see Figure 2.2). The infrastructure string portrays the
relevant factors for the change in content creation and market making by the process of digitization. The telecommunication industry,
payment providers, as well as the hardware and software industry are
players on the infrastructure string. The added value in DIS is portrayed on 3 stages looking at the 2 strings at the same time. Therefore, six core processes of value adding can be differentiated. Each of
these processes is further divided into relevant activities the players
might undertake (see Figure 2.3). For example, within the core process
"Content direction", the activities are "Content creation", like writing a professional article, but also the "Process of peer-reviewing" for
scientific journals, and the "Initiation of content creation", like the announcement of a special issue. The activities within one core process

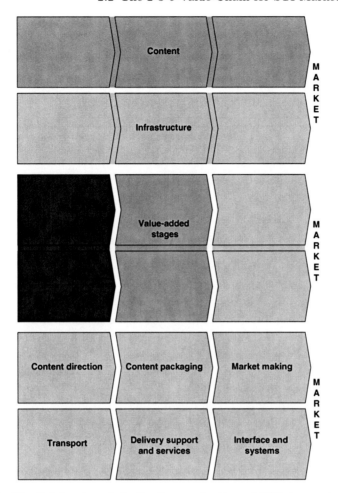

Fig. 2.2. The 2-3-6-value-chain for the production of STI: two strings, three stages, and six core processes of value adding activities (based on [SS97])

can be carried out by different players. Assigning the relevant activities to each player gives the role of this player in the market of STI. The determined roles should not be seen as static but undergoing a change depending on technical progress, cost structures, earning schemes, and the legal framework.

Focusing on the market of STI, the core processes of "Content direction", "Content packaging", "Market making", and "Delivery support and services" are the most relevant. The other two processes, "Transport" and "Interface and systems" are relevant factors for DIS but are mainly of importance in other areas like the telecommunication indus-

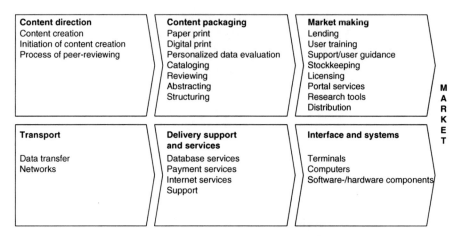

Fig. 2.3. The core processes with their relevant activities in the 2-3-6-value-chain

try or the hardware industry. Here, the industrial structure of these industries, especially their earning and cost structure, is taken as a given fact. Currently, there is no relevant independent software industry of recommender system software. Nearly all of the existing systems on the market are in house developments. Recommendation services fall into the core process of "Market Making". Depending on type, target users, and application they can play a significant role in "Portal services" and "Research tools".

2.3 The Strategic Positions of the Market Players

In the following the relevant activities of the players of STI markets are assigned to the processes of the 2-3-6-value-chain. The traditional domains are distinguished from the potential future activities, thereby portraying the shift from the current role within the market to the strategic position each player may take in the future. In some cases, the digitization together with the Internet as a new distribution channel has already lead to changes at some of the players. In these cases, still the traditional pre-digitization processes are defined in the value-chain but the ongoing shift is discussed in the text.

2.3.1 Authors in STI Markets

The process of content creation necessary for any further steps towards the market usually lies within the domain of the author, therefore the

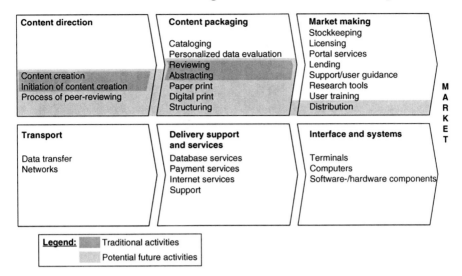

Fig. 2.4. The role of the author within the 2-3-6-value-chain

first player to be analyzed here. In Figure 2.4 the author's traditional activities are marked as well as the activities the author might be able to do in the future by means of digitization. The change resulting from technical progress is easily observed. Although the creation of content surely stays the central activity within the value-chain, the process of digitization makes other activities available. Authors today have the possibility of the electronic preparation of their own article and the immediate distribution of it with the help of the Internet, e. g. by a PDF-document on their website. However, besides other problems, this does neither solve the question of the estimation of the quality by users, nor the question, how users should be convinced of the article's relevance in the abundance of information on the Internet. "Portal services" and "Research tools" are none of the author's activities now or in the future, thus leaving the option of recommender systems blank. A single author generally does not have enough user traffic nor enough single documents to gain from the general advantages of a recommendation service.

2.3.2 Publishers in STI Markets

Traditionally publishing houses used to print their products on paper and earned their money by marketing them. The development of electronic distribution channels seems to be the biggest challenge for this industry. Figure 2.5 shows the potential future activities of publishers.

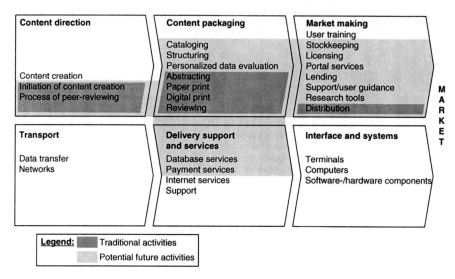

Fig. 2.5. The role of the publisher within the 2-3-6-value-chain

By means of digitization they can especially cover more processes in the area of "Market making". This can already be observed with the larger players of the industry, e. g. Elsevier with its online portal ScienceDirect[8] or Springer with SpringerLink[9]. These portals with their large quantity of documents and many users from academic institutions (holding an institutional license to these portals) are especially well suited areas for recommender systems. It is expected that they will include some type of recommendation service in the near future.

2.3.3 Bookstores in STI Markets

The bookselling trade is already undergoing a structural change right now, although so far it is not the digitization but the new distribution channel Internet that is of main concern (see in detail [ROW01]). Digital books are still a market niche since the bookstore and publishers do not favor such products due to problems concerning the digital rights management. Figure 2.6 points out the complete potential of the strategic options of bookstores including digital content. "Research tools" has always been a classic domain of bookstores, the future might bring an extension towards "Portal services". This can already by observed at Amazon.com. Amazon.com has been the most successful player taking

---

[8] http://www.sciencedirect.com
[9] http://www.springerlink.com

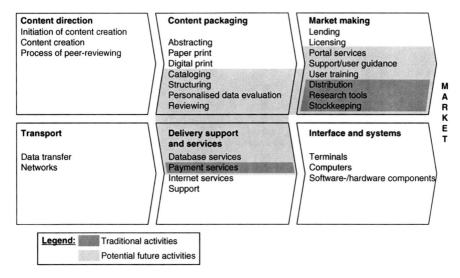

Fig. 2.6. The role of the bookstore within the 2-3-6-value-chain

advantage of the chance to new business models the Internet opened. The early introduction and wide range of recommender services at Amazon.com's first online store[10] (see [GGSHST02] for an overview) has been a strategic column of their market success. It will be analyzed in more detail in Section 4.3. Currently, most e-commerce bookstores (and competitors of Amazon.com, e.g. buch.de internetstores AG in Germany) are rushing to offer some kind of recommendation service.

2.3.4 Scientific Libraries in STI Markets

In Figure 2.7 it can be observed that scientific libraries are involved in three core processes: "Content packaging", "Market making", and "Delivery support and services". With the process of digitization going on, it still is not obvious, what the position of scientific libraries within STI markets should be and might be in the future. Preservation and categorization of their book inventory is the classical domain of libraries. Including digital content into the catalog today is mostly a question of copyright laws and digital rights management. What is of greater interest to this study is the market making. OPACs with their metadata text searches are the common research tools for scientific libraries. The following question needs to be resolved: Should scientific libraries be turned into customer oriented service portals that support the interaction of customers? Depending on the type, recommender systems can

---

[10] http://www.amazon.com

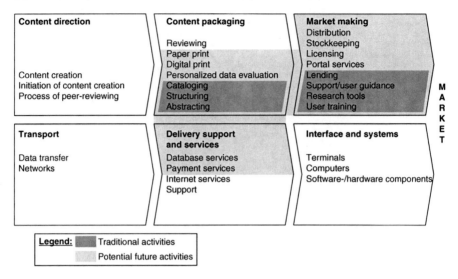

Fig. 2.7. The role of the scientific library within the 2-3-6-value-chain

be utilized as research tools for single users or as interaction platforms for the communication between users. Both approaches offer significant value-adding benefits to the libraries' patrons. The official mandate of state or university libraries should pronounce which approach should be taken.

2.3.5 Scientific Associations in STI Markets

The process of digitization enables larger associations to cover more processes closer to the market. Scientific associations can found their own publishing companies to self-market their created and reviewed content. A large potential of conflict with commercial publishers can be seen by comparing Figures 2.8 and 2.5. ACM and IEEE are two examples of large associations having founded their own publishing company including an online portal to its content: ACM operates ACM Portal[11] and IEEE runs IEEE Xplore[12]. These portals are taken up again in Section 4.1. With more technological advances, smaller associations are likely to follow. Recommender systems would add a significant value to such portals.

---

[11] http://portal.acm.org
[12] http://ieeexplore.ieee.org

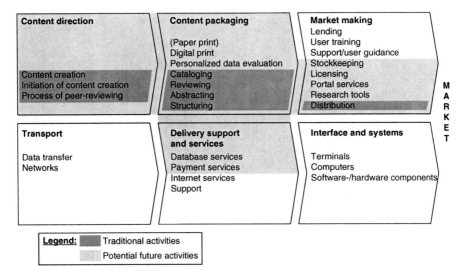

Fig. 2.8. The role of the scientific association within the 2-3-6-value-chain

2.4 Recommender Systems in the Business Profile of Information Providers

Comparing the traditional and future roles of the players in the last section it is obvious that all of them have the potential to broaden their activities towards the market side of the value chain. What is relevant for this study is the fact that authors, libraries, publishers, bookstores, and scientific associations might develop into strategic positions where their customers are the end users of scientific and technical information. These players—and also new possible entrants to the market—can try to take over activities in the core process of "Market making". All but the authors are coming into positions where they can drive the market or are being driven by market forces to offer advanced research tools and portal services to their customers. They compete on grounds where recommender systems are the tools of choice of many customers. In an ongoing competition, optimized research functions and portal services might be the central requirement for consumers for their decision to choose one or the other information provider. The combination of research function and the option of buying or loaning out will be a crucial point in the decision making process of the consumer on the Internet. Therefore, having the right combination of services in the portfolio is of great interest to any player to profit from the value added.

3

Classification and Mechanism Design of Recommender Systems

The success of a recommender system depends not only on the method of generating recommendations but upon the users' acceptance in various areas. In this chapter, different aspects of recommender systems that can serve as building blocks for different types and classifications of systems are determined. Depending on the goal, several classification schemes are possible. A classification based on the type of input data is presented in detail. The structure of the next chapters is derived from this classification.

Considering the customer service character of a recommender system, the overall mechanism of gathering and handling input from the customers is a key factor for success. With services whose mechanisms demand a strong user participation through some kind of automatic survey, the users must be motivated to actively participate and contribute truthfully to the system. Generally speaking, a recommender system can be interpreted as a static mechanism design game which belongs to the class of games of incomplete information. Depending on the choice of the mechanism, e. g. the type of the recommender system, several problems like bias or free riding might occur. In the second part of this chapter, the mechanism design problems—and solutions— for the different types of recommender systems are studied in more detail.

3.1 Classifications of Recommender Systems

This section presents a straight-forward classification of recommender systems. It is chosen to structure the remaining chapters of this book and to explain the different types of systems presented. Classification details that did not influence the design choices of the case studies in the next chapters are omitted. For more elaborated abstract classifications the reader is referred to the following papers: Resnick and Varian [RV97] present a classification of recommender systems based on the technical design as well as on the domain space of the service application. Focusing on e-commerce, a technical classification can be found in [SKR99] or [SKR01]. Adomavicius and Tuzhilin [AT05] give a more up-to-date overview on the generation of recommendation methods. [HKTR04] deals with the question of how to evaluate different types of recommender systems. An input/output-based classification of recommender systems including—as an example—a detailed analysis of the existing services at Amazon.com is presented in Gaul et al. [GGSHST02].

The approach used in this book is based to some extent on the input-data classification approach of Gaul et al. and to some extent on privacy issues. Three classification dimensions for recommender systems are relevant:

Explicit versus implicit input data. Explicit recommendations are based on direct user feedback. The input data of an explicit recommender system come from directly asking the users for their opinion on objects. Implicit recommendations are based on behavioral usage data as e. g. purchases, a user's browser session, or library lending data.

Degree of personalization. Observing or asking users for input is generally connected to some kind of identification of users; presenting recommendations to appropriate users makes it necessary to identify the appropriate ones. This identification can take place on different levels: Transaction or session level, pseudonyms, pseudonyms and attributes of the user, full identification, full identification and search context.

User-centered vs. item-centered. Most systems in e-commerce are built in a user-centered approach. Behavior or explicit input of preferences from users is gathered to classify the users into various groups on different levels according to their interests. This approach is favored from the sales point of view since it has the benefit of collecting valuable information for customer relationship management. Depending on the amount of available data, customers may well be classified down to groups of size one, allowing for one-to-one marketing. Nevertheless, this approach is not necessarily advantageous for both parties, privacy concerns may interfere with the participation on the customer side. When it comes to application areas with strong privacy concerns, item-centered recommender systems are the technique of choice. Here, anonymous users can be observed and their usage of items is stored and processed as item-to-item relations. User-centered recommender systems determine similarities between users and store user-to-user relations, item-centered systems determine relationships between items. The usage of item-centered services can be open anonymously to the general public without revealing one's own preferences besides the single object, one is currently inspecting.

Sometimes in the literature "content-based recommender systems" can be found and these are classified as a subgroup of implicit recommender systems. These systems in general cluster or classify objects based on their content or metadata descriptions. Content analysis includes e. g. automatic keyword extractions from scientific texts or automatic speech or text extraction and analysis from pictures, graphics, or videos. Metadata include product descriptions in consumers stores as well as full bibliographic data of library documents. The importance and usefulness of such retrieval tools is out of question. One of their advantages is that they are not prone to the mechanism design problems discussed in the next section. Some drawbacks of the content-based approach are known as well. Behavior-based recommender systems, as opposed to content-based systems, can work with legacy systems where no digital full text documents are available and where the metadata are incomplete. In addition, recommender systems can handle a multitude of object types in a uniform way. In the context of STI, this includes conventional books or journals, digital full texts, images, video or audio files, 3D models, and others. For the behavior-based system, it is sufficient to associate each object by a unique identifier, while a content-based system needs methods for similarity computation not only of objects of the respective type—which in itself is not trivial—but also for pairs of objects that do not share the same type. Behavior-based systems are language-independent and can easily integrate objects from different languages into the recommendation lists. Finally, content-based search and retrieval tools are not—lacking any kind of user participation—covered by the definition of recommender systems by Resnick and Varian given in Section 1.1 and thus are (with a few explicitly mentioned exceptions) not considered in the remainder of this book. Therefore, this work considers "implicit recommender system" to be a synonym for "behavior-based recommender system".

Explicit recommender systems are discussed in Chapter 5, while implicit—or behavior-based—recommender systems are the topic of Chapters 6 to 8.

3.2 Mechanism Design

The success of a recommender system critically depends upon the users' acceptance of the system. As has been shown above, the choice of the recommender mechanism implies considerable differences in the way that users interact with the system. It determines for instance the effort the user has to put into using the system and, even more critical, to contribute to it. For systems that demand a strong participation of the users, like explicit reviews, the users must be motivated to actively participate and contribute truthfully to the system.

The choice of the recommender system thus can be interpreted as a static mechanism design game which belongs to the class of games of incomplete information [FT95, pp. 243-318]. Optimal mechanisms have the property that agents participate voluntarily and that it is in their own best interest to behave truthfully. Such mechanisms are called incentive compatible. Unfortunately, however, often the combination of incomplete and asymmetric information leads to inefficient outcomes.

While a game theoretic formal analysis of this game is out of the scope of this contribution, a framework of stylized and simplified two-person games is presented which allow a qualitative discussion of the impacts of known mechanism design problems (bias, free riding, credibility, privacy, recognition, as well as feedback and network effects) for the classes of recommender systems introduced in the next chapters.

Here, the set of games comprises two classes of players, the operator of the recommender system and the users. The objective of the operator is to choose the recommender mechanism which maximizes the number of high-quality contributions with a given budget or, alternatively, to minimize his cost while keeping the system above a certain quality level. He may choose between explicit or behavior-based recommender mechanisms. Three classes of users can be distinguished, namely active and passive impartial users (e. g. students or researchers) and biased users (e. g. authors, editors, publishers, and their direct competitors). The operator, however, cannot observe the type of the user. Impartial users have the goal of minimizing their effort when using the mechanism or, alternatively, maximizing their utility from using the system. Biased users have the goal of maximizing their own utility or of minimizing the utility of their competitors, for instance in terms of book sales.

Users may choose between consuming recommendations, contributing truthfully to the system, and contributing in a biased way to the system.

Next, a short explanation of the known mechanism design problems listed above is given:

Bias (shilling). Bias in general refers to conscious or unconscious prejudice of the contributors. The most extreme form is shilling, where authors or publishers contribute glowing reviews and ratings for their own books and very negative reviews for the books of competitors.

Free riding. Free riding is due to the fact that recommendations are a public good which can be consumed by any user. However, as any public good, recommendations are in short supply because of the missing benefits for the authors of recommendations.

Credibility. Recommendations are only perceived as useful if they can be trusted. Users are very sensitive to credibility problems, e. g. when they realize that a supposedly objective review comes with a huge advertisement.

Privacy concerns versus recognition. On the one hand, it is often desirable to give active users some form of public recognition, like the inclusion into the list of the top n reviewers. On the other hand, users may choose to remain anonymous. Another problem concerning privacy is the revelation of interest of users to the public. This is a major concern for industrial research, because of its effect on competition.

Feedback effects. Feedback effects are known as path dependencies in nonlinear systems; this means that an early positive feedback may lead to a wide audience for a book while an early negative feedback may make this book to a failure in the market.

Network effects. With every user that contributes to the system, it becomes more useful, and therefore more attractive to other potential users.

Feedback and network effects are dynamic effects and occur only in repeated games.

Table 3.1 summarizes the mechanism design problems resulting from the operator's choice of mechanism. As can be seen, implicit, i. e. behavior-based, recommender systems have less problems than the explicit ones. The most important problem is that of obtaining a sufficiently large usage data set. This is called the cold start problem. But since most recommenders are added to an existing library system in order to complement the services of that system, it is possible to collect the desired data before the launch of the recommender application. Behavior-based recommender systems reveal preferences of users; in a competitive environment, this leads to privacy problems for users, and hence, to acceptance problems.

Table 3.1. The relevant mechanism design problems as a consequence of playing the stylized mechanism design game

User		Mechanism design problems	
User type	Action	Explicit Recommendations	Behavior-based Recommendations
Impartial passive	Consumption only	Free riding, network effects	—
Impartial active	Truthful contribution	Privacy	(Privacy)
Biased	Biased contribution	Bias, feedback, credibility	(Bias)

Explicit recommender systems are prone to biased recommendations, where documents are ranked or reviewed not according to their quality, but to other motives like acquaintance with the author. Equally, they have the problem of free riding, because users automatically profit from recommendations given by other users but must be motivated to write their own reviews due to the transaction costs of doing so. Credibility is a problem for explicit systems since recommendations might be filtered by the operator in order to suppress undesirable reviews or rankings. The credibility problem is much less pronounced in the scientific community, but the perceived credibility is mainly determined by the reputation of the organization offering the service. Considerable privacy concerns exist in these services, because in order to give public recognition to users, their (pseudonymous) identity must be revealed, which allows conclusions about their preferences. In explicit systems, feedback effects are quite pronounced. Reviews often depend on the reviews previously written, as these tend to influence the perception of the item and thus the judgment the user passes in the review.

Network effects are relevant to all recommender systems that are based on user input or behavior, although it is easier to attain a critical mass with behavior-based systems than with explicit ones.

As Avery stated, the market for evaluations is a specific one [ARZ99]; it is therefore crucial to implement an incentive system that takes into account the specific requirements for the users' motivation as well as the particular combination of problems that are relevant for the chosen mechanism. Optimally, users are intrinsically motivated to publish their opinion; in that case, no extrinsic motivation must be offered [Pre99]. An extrinsic motivation can take forms like payments for reviews, free goods, or public recognition on a review high score. However, for the operator extrinsic motivation systems may lead to an efficient provision of good recommendations (public goods), but it might be impossible for the operator to maintain a balanced budget at the same time, when individuals hide their true preferences to improve their individual welfare [Cla71, Gro73]. Payments and free goods on the one hand motivate users to contribute their reviews, and they may attract new users to join, but on the other hand, they may displace those users whose motives are altruistic and who, for instance, participate for the benefit of the scientific community. Unfortunately, it has been shown that experiments to measure these motivations correctly are very hard to accomplish [KP02].

Mechanism design problems are more prominent in explicit than in implicit recommender systems. In behavior-based systems free riding is almost not possible and creating bias deliberately in a system with web robot prevention has very high transaction costs and, therefore, is unattractive in many application areas. Whether a recommender system is operated as a stand-alone service or as a value-added service to an already high-frequented e-commerce site or library makes an essential difference. For stand-alone systems, the cold start problem of achieving a critical mass is the most important obstacle. At e-commerce or information sites like libraries all customers contribute to behavior-based systems helping to scale them up, regardless of their interest and usage of the recommendation service itself.

Recognition of good cooperation within explicit systems can be measured by reputation systems (even for credence goods [Emo97]). A user point account tracks useful and undesirable behavior and adds credit or deducts points, respectively. An automatic decrease in points (discounting) over time is necessary to keep customers motivated to contribute. Desirable und undesirable behavior, for example, can be measured by the textual quality of reviews; this quality again can be measured by ratings from other users for this review.

Credibility is a crucial point for the long-run success of a recommendation service. In the academic environment the credibility of a library's recommender service comes to a large part from the reputation of the institution it belongs to. If sales promotions or advertisements of any kind within the main platform (online store, library, etc.) exist, a customer should experience a clear separation between these and the recommender system. In e-commerce applications like Amazon.com this is often not the case: product managers place products with a high contribution to profit next to real recommendations from other customers.

Shilling of recommender systems by outsiders (not the operator but other "customers") is often a sign of faulty mechanism design. How shilling can be done technically for various recommendation generating algorithms is shown in [LR04]. Producers (e. g. authors) often wish to influence the systems to recommend their own products. The possibility to anonymously submit contributions—e. g. ratings or reviews—and thereby pushing one's own product (or discrediting competitors) is a significant incentive that can lead to a large amount of contributions in e-commerce. In the short-run such false recommendations are often welcome by e-retailers to increase the revenue, in the long run they discredit the credibility of all recommendations.

4

A Survey of Recommender Systems at Major STI Providers

The usage of recommender systems at major STI providers is still in its infancy. This chapter gives an overview of the existing recommendation services at scientific libraries, some of the relevant scientific projects, as well as the most relevant e-commerce application for STI. A comparable analysis can be found in [FGSN08]. While the quantity—not necessarily the quality as well—of recommender systems in commercial applications is quite high, very few scientific recommender research groups have their own permanently running services open to the general public. Although nearly all traditional scientific libraries at large universities have been turned into hybrid libraries covering both paper and digital documents, more advanced research tools besides standard database metadata searches do not exist often. Purely digital libraries of large scientific associations are currently beginning to experiment with recommender systems. Many of the new research tools are based on content analysis and feature user interfaces similar to the ones used by recommender systems for the presentation. Therefore, for comparison purposes, some content-based services are discussed in this chapter as well, even if they do not fulfill the definition of a recommender system from Section 1.1.

4.1 Scientific Libraries

When browsing through the Open Public Access Catalogs (OPACs) of Europe's national libraries which are members of The European Library[1] (formerly Gabriel, the portal of European national libraries that has been funded by the European Union) and the OPAC of the

---

[1] http://www.theeuropeanlibrary.org

U.S. American Library of Congress, not a single operational recommender system can be found. However, some scientific digital libraries are already experimenting with such systems. Unfortunately—and contrarily to Amazon.com where at least the general principles behind the behavior-based recommender have been published—the digital libraries of the scientific organizations discussed here, ACM Portal and IEEE Xplore, do not reveal the principles and algorithms employed in their recommender services. Therefore, the description of these services here is limited mainly to the characteristics perceived by the user.

4.1.1 ACM Portal

The ACM portal[2] incorporates an implicit non-personalized recommendation service as well as a content-based research tool.

The content-based system analyzes the text of research papers. The service is available on the detail page for each document, where the link "Find similar Articles" causes the system to search for related articles. According to the announcement by White [Whi01], the "algorithms used for Similar searches are not obvious, but involve the use of dictionaries, thesauri, and cluster analysis of full-text indices." The results are ranked according to their title, publication, date, publisher, or relevance, but there is no information available as to how exactly this relevance measure is computed.

The behavior-based recommender system can be found at the bottom of the document detail page under the heading "Peer to Peer – Readers of this Article have also read". At the time of writing, this recommendation service seemed less useful than the content-based one, as many of the recommendation lists contained a paper on data structures for quadtree approximation or another paper titled "constructing reality". Thus, it is conjectured, that it is based on a simple frequency count of the items and does not filter random occurrences from the usage history as described in Section 7.1. Furthermore, given the apparent size of the set of recommended articles, the recommender seems to be a relatively new addition to the ACM digital library whose performance might improve as the size of the observed data set increases.

4.1.2 IEEE Xplore

The IEEE Xplore site[3] currently has no recommender application on their production site. There exists, however, a system under develop-

---

[2] http://portal.acm.org
[3] http://ieeexplore.ieee.org/

ment that can be reached via the IEEE e-Workshop page[4] which at the time of writing this study delivered empty lists. According to Grenier [Gre05] the system will be content-based, but no further algorithmic details are given.

4.1.3 CiteSeer

CiteSeer[5] [GBL98] originally started as an internal research project at NEC Research Institute. It has implemented several ways to find and recommend related documents. The current version only contains non-personalized services, although in the first publications [BLG00] the authors still presented personalized services based on account information. While the reasons for the withdrawal of personalized services are not published, this might either be due to the scalability problems when moving from a restricted corporate environment to a global web service or to the reluctance of Internet users to use personal accounts for their research tasks.

CiteSeer's recommendation services or related content-based tools basically fall into three classes:

Link structure based. Four relations based on the citation link structure are exploited to derive recommendations for a given document:

Documents that are cited by the document. This is a classical strategy in literature search, but it is restricted to the past as a document can only include those that temporally preceded it.

Documents that cite the document. This relation is the inverse of the former and helps finding works that build upon the findings of the document.

Co-citations. This group includes all documents that are cited together with the document in publications.

Active bibliography. These documents cite the same publications as the document.

These four approaches exhaustively search the direct neighborhood of a document, but ignore anything that has a higher distance than two in terms of hops in the citation network. Although the more advanced methods for instance by Brin et al. [PBMW98] are mentioned in [LGB99], they are currently not implemented.

Content-based. These limitations do not apply to the lists generated by the content-based methods; these results are summarized under

---

[4] http://research.ieeexplore.ieee.org/research/search.jsp
[5] http://citeseer.ist.psu.edu

the headings "Similar documents (at the sentence level)" and "Similar documents based on text". According to the developers [LGB99], these lists are compiled using a weighted sum of TF-IDF (Term Frequency / Inverse Document Frequency) of word vectors, distance computation between the documents' headers using LikeIt [Yia97], and a measure called CCIDF (Common Citation × Inverse Document Frequency) that uses the references analogously to TF-IDF. The TF-IDF measure [SY73] originates from information retrieval. It is used to determine the importance of a term for a document. The term frequency (TF) is defined as the number of occurrences of a term in a document, normalized by the number of all term occurrences in that document. The inverse document frequency (IDF) is a measure of the importance of a term in a corpus of documents; it is the logarithm of the quotient of the number of all documents and the number of documents containing the term. The TF-IDF measure is given as the fraction $\frac{TF}{IDF}$.

Explicit. In addition, the site offers its users the possibility of rating a paper on a scale from 1 to 5, and to additionally enter comments, i. e. short reviews, on the paper.

4.1.4 Google Scholar

Google Scholar[6] uses a function for finding related articles that resembles the similar pages feature offered by the Google search engine. The service is based on an analysis of the content of the documents and ,according to the help pages, the results are ranked according to their similarity to the document for which the recommendations were requested as well as to the relevance of the paper derived from the Page-Rank of the respective document [PBMW98]. Furthermore, it is possible to search for documents that cited the document of interest, but documents cited by it cannot be retrieved via Google Scholar. Google Scholar is also used e. g. by JSTOR[7] in a way similar to that in which the Google search engine is embedded in other sites, to provide similar publications.

---

[6] http://scholar.google.com
[7] http://www.jstor.org

4.2 Scientific Projects

4.2.1 TechLens

The TechLens[8] recommender is an extension of the known collaborative filtering GroupLens system [RIBR94] to the domain of scientific papers. Motivated by the flood of scientific publications in all domains, the system integrates different content-based filtering (CBF) and collaborative filtering (CF) approaches [MAC+02, TMA+04] into hybrid approaches. The objective of collaborative filtering is to make predictions about the opinion a user will express concerning a given item based on the judgments of other, similar users about that item. Judgments are usually given as ratings on a numerical scale, and the similarity between users is defined as the similarity of past ratings submitted by the users. The idea behind collaborative filtering is that users who have expressed a similar taste in the past tend to agree on similar ratings in the future.

The two methods from collaborative filtering included in the system work on the citation graph, where papers are interpreted as customers, and the citation links that they contain are seen as recommendations for the cited papers. The similarity of two papers is then defined as the share of common citations. The first idea, Pure CF, is to build a k-nearest neighbors CF system that generates recommendations for a paper based on its citations, using the recommendations, i.e. citations, from the k most similar papers. The second, Denser CF, goes one step further by using the citations of the citations in the original paper as input.

The CBF methods rely on the TF-IDF measure on the papers' titles and abstracts that are submitted to Porter's stemming algorithm [Por80]. The first one, Pure CBF calculates the similarity of the paper to other papers and recommends the most similar ones. In addition, CBF Separated also considers the text of the papers the current paper cites, generates recommendations for each of these papers, and then merges the recommendation lists in order to recommend the papers with the highest similarity scores. Finally, CBF Combined first merges the titles and abstracts of the current paper and the papers cited by it before identifying the papers with the highest similarity to the merged text.

Different hybrid algorithms are assembled from these building blocks: CF-CBF Separated, CF-CBF Combined, CBF Separated-CF, and CBF Combined-CF. All of these use the first algorithm in their

---

[8] http://techlens.cs.umn.edu/tl3

name to generate input for the second one that generates recommendations for each of the first-level recommendations and ranks them. The fusion algorithm, on the other hand, runs both CF and CBF in parallel. Those papers that appear in both recommendation lists are sorted according to the sum of their ranks in these lists, the other papers are appended to the combined list.

As experiments have shown, the quality of the recommendations depends on the nature of the paper for which recommendations are sought. For instance, novel material can best be found in the CiteSeer data set used for the evaluation by either Pure CF or the Fusion method, whereas recommendations on introductory papers are best obtained from CBF Separate or CF-CBF Separate.

4.2.2 The Melvyl Recommender Project

The Melvyl recommender project [WS06] initiated by the California Digital Library aimed at using both analysis of circulation data of documents and content-based methods exploiting terms from bibliographic records. The circulation data used by the project contain pseudonymous identification numbers for each patron of the library that allow to track purchases in the sense of checked out physical items. Digital content purchases are not included in the data set.

Whitney et al. [WS06] have identified a number of problems, e. g. data sparsity and privacy concerns of the patrons, when using standard collaborative filtering methods. This motivated them to pursue an itemto-item approach. A similarity graph is constructed from the purchase histories using documents as nodes and the number of common purchases as edge weights. The recommendations for a given document are generated by identifying all neighbors of the document and sorting them according to the edge weights. Since results were of varying quality, they were filtered according to an adapted classification scheme from the library in order to remove unrelated recommendations. This procedure, though, always entails the danger of removing potentially interesting items from other disciplines.

4.3 E-Commerce: Amazon.com

Amazon.com's website has been, for the last years, the most prominent example for the integration of information services, especially recommendation and personalization, into a commercial website and as such has deserved a closer consideration. Especially two services will be detailed here: the explicit and the implicit recommender system. An overview of the other recommender services on the site around the year 2001 can be found in [GGSHST02].

The implicit recommender ("Customers Who Bought This Item Also Bought") is based on the principles published in the article by Linden et al. [LSY03] and various patents held by the company [LJB01]. It relies on item-to-item collaborative filtering by recommending items that are similar to objects that have attracted the customer's attention. Products of interest are those items that the user either has bought in the past, has currently in the shopping cart, has rated, or products whose detail pages the customer is inspecting. The motivation to deviate from the more classical user-to-user collaborative filtering was mainly motivated by scalability considerations, since Linden et al. [LSY03] claim that the existing algorithms do not scale to the order of magnitude of Amazon.com's product and customer data bases. This implies that, as the patent claim states, the similarity between items is not user specific, but general. The similarity measure may for instance be computed as the cosine between the purchase vectors of each pair of items. The recommender then chooses those items that have the highest similarity. For binary entries in the purchase matrix (customer has bought the item or not), this is equivalent to recommending the items that have been bought most frequently together with the article in which the customer is interested. Linden et al. name as main advantage of this algorithm its scalability that, coupled with a massive amount of offline computation of similarities, allows a fast generation of recommendations for each of the several million articles offered by Amazon.com. Contrarily to the behavior-based recommender system presented in Section 8 of this work, the Amazon.com recommender is not able to distinguish between random, independent co-purchases that have no significance, and meaningful co-purchases that are due to dependent purchase processes.

The explicit recommender system allows users to rate items using a short rating of one to five stars on the one hand and a textual review on the other. This is done at the same time on the same web page. By this design, the ratings are considered as a tool to present the overall opinion detailed in the textual review; the ratings are generally used to sort the reviews for display purposes. Contrarily to the explicit recommender system presented in Chapter 5, at Amazon.com reviews and rankings are two features of one service, not two independent services. Active reviewers are incentivized for instance with badges for the top n reviewers or shopping coupons.

Item-to-recommendation relations at Amazon.com are obviously based on some fuzzy title-based concept. Ratings and reviews contributed to a specific product are also displayed at products with a close relationship in the title. A book review written for the hardcover edition might also be helpful for the paperback. Presenting reviews of an older edition at the product page of an updated and extended edition of a scientific book is questionable at least. At Amazon.com not only are reviews of older editions shifted to new ones but vice versa without making this process visible to the user. Very misleading results are produced by this item-to-recommendation identification mechanism when it comes to positive title correlations between products of different media formats. Anyone who was once disappointed about the movie adaption of his favorite novel understands that it is not a good idea to automatically transfer reviews between books, radio plays, or even movie DVDs. Presenting as much reviews as possible to any product seems to be the main criteria for Amazon.com.

The main motivation behind the use of personalization and recommendation services is that the conversion rates of the recommended items are considerably larger than those advertised via untargeted ads. The downside of this is the high incentive for shilling, which has already been discussed in Section 3.2. In the last years at various occasions Amazon.com has ascertained that different services at their website have been abused.[9] The possibility for everybody—including authors and publishers—to anonymously submit reviews or ratings and thereby pushing one's own product or discrediting competitors seems to be a significant incentive that has lead to the large amount of reviews at Amazon.com. Recently, this mechanism design has started to discredit the credibility of all recommendations and thereby the positive attitude of the customers towards the service. After some negative publicity Amazon.com has changed the mechanism design so that only customers who have purchased at least one item with the according account can submit reviews. In other countries (e. g. Germany with Amazon.de[10]) the mechanism design is still different. Here, reviews can still be submitted from new (fake) accounts without prior purchases (status of 2007-05-03).

---

[9] http://news.com.com/2100-1023-976435.html, http://www.wired.com/techbiz/media/news/2002/07/53634, http://query.nytimes.com/gst/fullpage.html?res=9C07E0DC1F3AF937A25751C0A9629C8B63&scp=1&sq=Amazon.com%20canadian&st=cse

[10] http://www.amazon.de

4.4 Social Tagging

Social websites are the most recent trend in the media industry. They include user-centric publishing, like wikis and blogs, and social resource sharing tools. Websites like Flickr, del.icio.us[11], YouTube, MySpace[12], and Wikipedia[13] have flourished and caught the attention of the media industry. The main reasons for the success of these social web sites is the opportunity of participation without special skills and without overhead for every individual. Social websites have attracted a huge number of individual users which have created huge amounts of content in these websites within a very short period of time. It seems that social websites effectively handle the knowledge acquisition problem by attracting huge masses of active users. Tags are user created metadata of items. The determination of items with similar tag clouds gives way to item-centered recommender systems; classifying users by their contributed tags leads to user-centered systems. In this section, three services in the area of STI are portrayed and analyzed.

4.4.1 BibSonomy and CiteULike

In social websites, in addition to content- or behavior-based structures, information on the social web between users becomes available and is exploited for giving recommendations. In a scientific library setting BibSonomy[14] [HJSS06] is an experimental social bookmark and publication sharing system which investigates how the social structure can contribute towards deriving good recommendations. At the core of BibSonomy is the formal definition of a folksonomy as a quintuple of users, tags, resources, the ternary tag assignment relation between users, tags, and resources, and a user-specific subtag-supertag relation which defines a user-specific hierarchy of tags. While ignoring the subtag-supertag relation, a folksonomy falls back on the ternary tag assignment relation which can be interpreted as a triadic context in formal concept analysis and interpreted as a tripartite undirected hypergraph with three types of vertices, namely users, tags, and resources, and the set of hyperedges defined by the ternary tag assignment relation. Tag assignments can be easily augmented with other attributes like date, user group, or resource type which define an extended context of the structure.

---

[11] http://del.icio.us
[12] http://www.myspace.com
[13] http://www.wikipedia.org
[14] http://www.bibsonomy.org

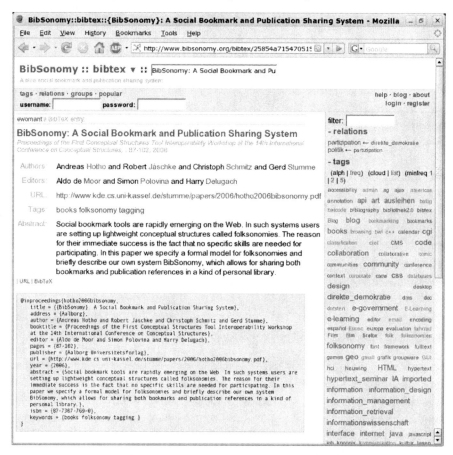

Fig. 4.1. The BibSonomy entry for [HJSS06]

Figure 4.1 shows BibSonomy's detail page for the contribution by Hotho et al. [HJSS06]. In addition to browsing the bibliographic data, the user can follow different links. The tag cloud on the right hand side of the screen shows the tags users have associated with the current document. Clicking on a tag either in the tag cloud or in the list displayed with the bibliographic information leads to the document owner's entry page, filtered for resources that are correspondingly tagged. Clicking on the author link leads to a page displaying the resource that also have this author on their author lists.

CiteULike[15] pursues an approach of social tagging similar to Bib-Sonomy. It also supports tags and allows to follow links for tags, authors, as well as the users that have a document in their library. Both

---

[15] http://www.citeulike.org

sites alleviate the task of entering the bibliographic information by offering an import plugin from selected sites like e. g. CiteSeer or IEEE Explore. The United-Kingdom-based CiteULike started the service in 2004, even before the Germany-based BibSonomy.

4.4.2 LibraryThing

LibraryThing[16] is another social cataloging web application for storing and sharing personal library catalogs and book lists that started in 2005. It offers recommendations based on the tag clouds of users. In general, the document data has to be imported by the users. It mainly is a service that lives through its own portal, but tries to spread its output through other institutions.

LibraryThing is commercially offering its data to libraries for use in local library catalogs. Figure 4.2 shows the integration within the OPAC of the J. Paul Leonard Library at San Francisco State University. One problem arises with this approach: the user base is separated from the contributor base. All input data stems from the LibraryThing website. The community of users at the LibraryThing website generates tags and recommendations suited for their interest and background. The user group at a library that shows the output of LibraryThing most likely differs from the LibraryThing contributor base. Recommendations are most useful for a peer group if they are created from the input of the same peer group. A user at a fine arts university gets the same LibraryThing-recommendations for an interdisciplinary book as a student at a technical college in case both their institutional libraries integrated the LibraryThing recommendations. Both users might prefer different recommendations from their peer group. Nevertheless, the approach of LibraryThing has one important positive aspect: a community at a single library is often too small to achieve critical mass for a successful recommendation service.

A second drawback of this approach is that the tag clouds that emerge at social websites seem to be less useful than the classification systems developed by scientific communities (e. g. the Mathematics Subject Classification[17] or the ACM Computing Classification System[18])—at least for STI providers.

---

[16] http://www.librarything.com
[17] http://www.ams.org/msc
[18] http://www.acm.org/class

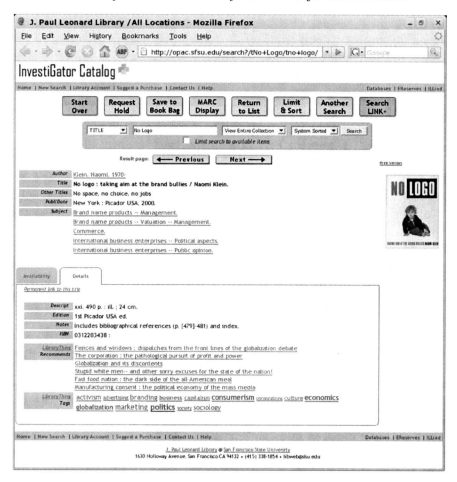

Fig. 4.2. LibraryThing recommendations and tags added to the document details at the J. Paul Leonard Library at San Francisco State University

5

Case Study: Explicit Recommender Services for Scientific Libraries

In March 2006, a group-specific item-centered explicit recommender system featuring a rating and a review service was added to the OPAC of the Library of the Universität Karlsruhe (TH). The goal is to turn the online public access catalogs of libraries into customer oriented service portals including the support of customer interaction. In this chapter, the services are described, usage statistics are given, and the question, which type of recommender system is appropriate for which customer need, is covered. The mechanism design of the recommender systems is discussed as well as possible extensions to the current implementation. A description of these services was first published in [Neu07a].

5.1 General Setup

In the scientific world the organized exchange about the quality of a publication is usually performed by dedicated survey and review journals, where domain experts discuss and review the publication and give a state-of-the-art survey of a certain specialized research topic, e. g. ACM Computing Surveys and ACM Computing Reviews in the field of computer science. The introduction of explicit recommender systems heralds a change in this system. Review journals require a conscious effort to locate the review for a publication, an effort that not every user is willing to spend, especially if reading the review implies the monetary costs of buying the journal. Explicit recommender systems, on the other hand, are integrated into the OPAC and thus deliver the information to the user at minimal costs for the user. In addition, at least for books that receive broad public attention, many reviews and publications are produced by their readers which reduces the influence that a single review has on the user's purchase decision.

Libraries are an application area with strong privacy concerns, therefore, item-centered recommender systems are the technique of choice. The usage of recommendations is open anonymously to the general public without revealing one's own preferences besides the single object, one is currently inspecting. While the item-centered approach has some limitations when it comes to determine the users' overall interest, many scientific libraries refrain from collecting document browsing or lending histories of individual users. The recent interest of politicians in this data for dragnet investigation and the knowledge of scientists about it would most likely influence the scientific freedom at the institution the specific library belongs to.

In the portrayed item-centered recommender systems the customer interaction takes place around the library's objects. This constraint can be regarded as strength. The interacting library users build a social network, but they do not just connect to each other, they connect through a shared object. This object is the reason and the necessity for the connection. It is a case of object-centered sociology [SKCvS01].

In March 2006 a rating service and a review service were introduced together at the University Library of Karlsruhe[1]. Inspecting ratings and reviews is open to the general public, submitting ratings and writing reviews is only open to logged-in users to prevent fraudulent use. The account to log in comes with the possession of a library card only. The difference to most other systems lies, first, in the support of different user and target groups and second, on a role system based on scientific experience, where the roles are reliably determined and tracked by the library administration. Most other applications are based on less reliable self-assessment for the determination of user groups. For example, [GSHJ01] presents an early application of group-specific behavior-based recommendation services based on self-assessment in e-learning. With the services portrayed in this chapter, the user group of the rater or reviewer is stored and processed with each rating and review; different reviews for different target groups can be submitted for each catalog object from each user. In the current implementation three different user groups exist: students (Studenten), university staff (Mitarbeiter), and externs (Externe) officially not directly associated with the university. Although scientific staff is not distinguishable from administrative staff in this way it is obvious from the work tasks that the staff group is actually a close approximation of all scientists at the Universität Karlsruhe (TH). These groups are chosen for legacy reasons. They have been used by the library administration for many years preceding these services;

---

[1] http://www.ubka.uni-karlsruhe.de

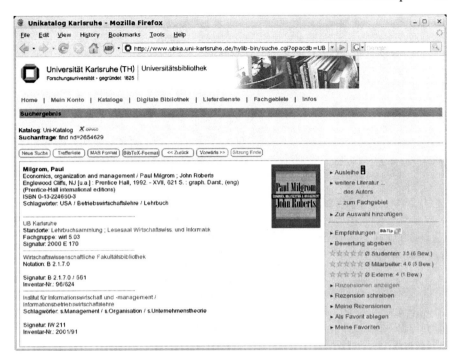

Fig. 5.1. Detailed inspection page

they are not only checked for each customer before handing out the library card but also tracked over time in case of status changes. While one could easily come up with more sophisticated classifications, the guaranteed correctness made these user groups the pragmatic choice for a system with an existing customer base of roughly 25,000 customers.

All presented systems are fully operational services accessible by the general public in the online catalog of the University Library of Karlsruhe (UBKA – Universitätsbibliothek Karlsruhe)[2]. Further information on how to use these services can be found at "Participate!" at the scientific projects website[3]. The library's documents covered by the services include digital and paper books and journals, various data mediums, as well as picture, audio and video files.

As a starting point to all services the detailed inspection page of a library document was chosen. None of the services has an exclusive starting page; first, one has to choose an object to see the respective recommendations. The general research work flow starts with entering search words into the traditional database oriented OPAC search page.

---

[2] http://www.ubka.uni-karlsruhe.de/catalog
[3] http://reckvk.em.uni-karlsruhe.de

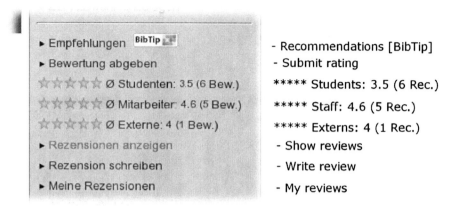

Fig. 5.2. Enlarged cutout of the detailed document inspection page showing the user front end of the recommendation services

This results in getting a list of documents with short titles, author, and year of publication. Choosing one document from the list displays the detailed document inspection page. Figure 5.1 shows this page for "Economics, organization and management" by Milgrom and Roberts [MR92]. The recommender system information can be found in the colored box on the right hand side next to the cover image. Unfortunately, the OPAC is only available in German. Figure 5.2 shows an enlarged cutout of this area with an English translation next to it. The recommendation services are accessible by clicking on the links: "Recommendations [BibTip]" displays behavior-based recommendations as described in Chapter 8; "Submit rating" opens the submission page for document ratings; "Show reviews" opens the page for browsing user reviews for the document; "Write review" opens the editing page for document reviews; "My reviews" opens a page for the management of all reviews written by the current user. Rating averages for the three user groups can be directly inspected at the stars. Only suitable links are shown, if no reviews or behavior-based recommendations exist, the respective links are omitted. If one is not logged in, the login page is displayed before the various submission and editing pages.

The services described in this chapter are developed in an AJAX (Asynchronous JavaScript and XML) like technique, programmed in PHP facilitating the DOM (Document Object Model) and JavaScript, use PostgreSQL databases, and are running on Linux servers.

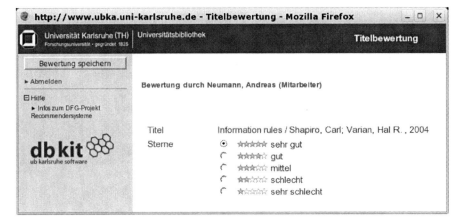

Fig. 5.3. Submission page for document ratings

5.2 Rating Service

The rating service was set up to give the customers a tool for a first quick estimation of the overall quality of a document within certain user groups. A rating for a library object can be submitted by a logged-in user on a Likert scale from 1 (very bad) to 5 (very good). The submission page is reached via the link "Bewertung abgeben – Submit rating" on the detailed document inspection page (conf. Figures 5.1 and 5.2). The submission interface for the title "Information rules" by Shapiro and Varian is shown in Figure 5.3. In bold font the name of the current user is shown: "Bewertung durch... – Rating by...". The possible rating values are explicitly shown including the star graphics:

- 5 stars – sehr gut – very good
- 4 stars – gut – good
- 3 stars – mittel – average
- 2 stars – schlecht – bad
- 1 star – sehr schlecht – very bad

Every user can rate every document only once. The ratings are processed separately for each customer group and shown in aggregated form. In Figure 5.2 6 ratings from students with an average of 3.5 stars, 5 ratings from staff with an average of 4.6 stars, and 1 from the group of externs with a good (4 stars) rating can be seen. Therefore, the book of Milgrom and and Roberts seems to be an overall good book at first glance, which is even more valued by scientists than by students.

Fig. 5.4. Editing page for reviews

5.3 Review Service

The review service was introduced to give the library's customers a tool to manage detailed information about the content, the quality, and the adequacy of a document for a specific task, e. g. preparation for a student's examination. This is especially helpful when the library object is not digitally available through the OPAC. Browsing the information of this service takes significantly longer than with the rating service and should be used if the customer already considers the document potentially useful. The system is designed in the following way. Every logged-in user can submit four different reviews for each library document, one for the target group of students (Studenten), one for university staff (Mitarbeiter), one for externs (Externe), and an additional one not assigned to any target group (nicht zugeordnet). By means of this, special characteristics of a document can be considered. Parts of a book may be well suited for a specific course (target group of students), while other aspects of the same book are more valued by scientists, e. g. the list of references or chapters on advanced material.

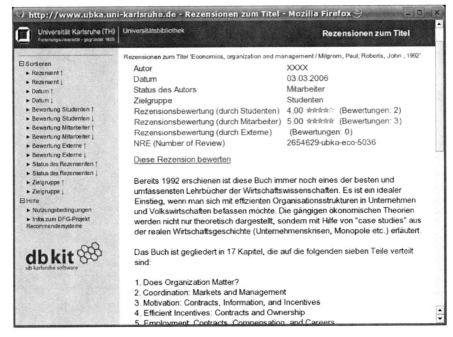

Fig. 5.5. Browsing page for reviews

Figure 5.4 shows the editing page for reviews for the book (Werk) "Service management and marketing" by Grönroos [Grö05]. The review author has to choose a target group (Zielgruppe) and to decide whether his real name should appear with the review (Anonymitätsgrad – degree of anonymity). Reviews can be managed (written, edited, deleted, saved) within the system over several sessions, only after explicitly releasing them (Freigabestatus – status of release) they become visible to others. Terms of use (Nutzungsbedingungen) are shown, but no automatic check from library staff is included in the workflow of submitting a review. Every reader can report offending reviews but no such case has occurred so far. In such a case, the review will be deleted and the author will be contacted. The service management knows every reviewer even if one chooses not to show one's real name with the review.

Additionally, a rating service with reviews as the central objects is provided. Thereby, readers of a review can give feedback about the quality of the review. The user group handling and presentation in this review rating service is implemented similar to the service built around the library documents presented in the previous section.

The browsing page for reviews is shown in Figure 5.5. The author (Autor) chose to stay anonymous (**XXXX**) , the review was submitted

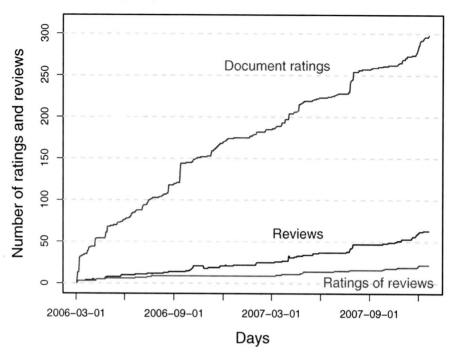

Fig. 5.6. Number of document ratings, reviews, and ratings of reviews online for the general public in the OPAC from 2006-03-03 to 2007-12-20

on 2006-03-03, the author belongs to the staff group (Mitarbeiter), and the target group is students (Studenten), it has been rated (Rezensionsbewertung) two times by students with an average of 4.0 (good) and three times by scientists with an average of 5.0 (very good). On the left hand side various sorting criteria (up and down) for reviews exist: reviewer (Rezensent), date (Datum), ratings (Bewertung) from the different user groups, reviewer group (Status des Rezensenten), as well as target group. More reviews for this title can be found by scrolling down.

5.4 Usage Statistics

In this section, usage statistics of the explicit recommendation services at the Library of the Universität Karlsruhe (TH) are given. The discussion, i.e. mechanism design problems that may have an influence on these numbers, technical issues, and an outlook how to push the usage of the different services, follows in the next section.

Table 5.1. Number of contributions by user group (status of 2007-12-20)

	Students	Researchers	Externs	Total
Document ratings	148	116	34	298
Reviews	29	21	13	63
Ratings of reviews	11	11	0	22

Table 5.2. Number of ratings by rating value (status of 2007-12-20)

	Very bad	Bad	Average	Good	Very good
Document ratings	5	9	29	91	164
Ratings of reviews	0	1	3	9	9

Table 5.3. Number of reviews by target group (status of 2007-12-20)

	Students	Researchers	Externs	Not assigned
Target group of review	19	4	2	38

Figure 5.6 shows the history of the total number of document ratings, released reviews, and ratings of reviews online from 2006-03-03 to 2007-12-20. The total number as well as the distribution of all contributions by the three user groups on the last day of this time period is portrayed in Table 5.1. Table 5.2 depicts the distribution by rating values of document ratings and ratings of reviews. Table 5.3 shows the distribution of reviews by target group.

5.5 Discussion

5.5.1 Usage and Mechanism Design

Although recommender systems are clearly beneficial to users, scientific libraries have been slow compared to e-commerce to introduce such systems as regular features in their OPACs. To the best of knowledge, the presented recommendation services were the first of their respective kind at large scientific libraries and have received positive feedback from the library community. Nevertheless, the overall amount of user contributions is still low although constantly growing (conf. Figure 5.6). The small number of contributions can be attributed in different parts to the general size of the potential contributor group, free riding, the non-visibility of the services due to a lack of marketing, and technical issues in the user interface.

When users decide to contribute, they are obviously more interested in recognizing good books and reviews than in marking bad ones (conf.

Table 5.2). Table 5.1 shows the tendency that the system is accepted best within the group of researchers, considering that the total number of persons in this group is significantly smaller than in the student group.

The explicit recommender systems at the University Library of Karlsruhe in the current setup are designed to prevent shilling from outsiders. The large downturn is the limitation of the amount of potential contributors. A service run through its own portal open to all Internet users most likely has an even smaller conversation rate of turning visitors into contributors, but the final amount of contributions will be much higher. This favors an approach like LibraryThing (conf. Section 4.4.2). Clicking in the OPAC on cover images like the one seen in Figure 5.1 on page 45 brings the library user directly to the corresponding page at Amazon.de. Although by means of this mechanism a one click connection from the inspection of ratings and reviews to e-retail exists and the intersection of the set of university staff and the set of authors of library documents is not empty, currently self promotion of authors seems not to be present, the credibility is not challenged so far. The size limitation of the group of potential reviewers as well as the lack of extrinsic motivation are two important aspects for the slow growth of ratings and reviews.

Contrarily to Amazon.com a non-fuzzy item-to-recommendation relationship is used. Ratings or reviews are not automatically shifted to other editions or documents with a strong correlation in the title. While this limits the visibility of reviews, it produces no misleading results as can be often found at Amazon.com (conf. Section 4.3). This should help to build up trust in the usefulness of the recommender system at the University Library of Karlsruhe.

5.5.2 Technical Issues

One technical problem of the current implementation that influences the usage of the service in a negative way is the fact that customers searching the catalog are normally not logged in. The majority of paper documents in the library is available via open access; one only has to log in to order in advance an already lent book or an older book from the depot. The hurdle of first logging in seems too much of a hassle for many users for submitting ratings. Currently, the login mechanism of the recommendation service is even separated from the general OPAC login. When a user is already logged in into the OPAC—as it is then already clearly stated on the website on all pages in his session—and gets a second request to log in without any explanation, this is often considered as an error and the transaction is stopped before finalizing the contribution. This has been stated repeatedly from first-time users and can be found in the usage statistics as well. From 2007-01-01 to 2007-12-21 the link "Submit rating" has been clicked 949 times; 123 ratings have been submitted within this period. This shows that only in about 1 out of 8 clicks the users make the effort to log in and give a rating.

Another technical issue lies in the pop-up-based interface. After the extensive use of pop-up advertisements on various websites and the spread of pop-up-blockers on the consumer side in the Internet, most service operators have switched back to one-window-only interfaces and successfully regained customer confidence. In the OPAC of the university library, a click on any of the links to display reviews, submit a review, submit a rating, or browse one's own reviews always opens a new browser window (conf. Figures 5.3, 5.4, and 5.5 on pages 47, 48, and 49, respectively) cluttering up screen space. This has been reported by several users as an annoyance.

Furthermore, the visibility of a service is essential for its usage. Amazon.com e. g. displays recommendations directly on the product page. The recommendation service gets into the eye of every customer even if the customer was completely unaware of it before. At the Library of the Universität Karlsruhe (TH) the reviews are accessible via a single link that is only displayed if reviews are available. The review link is one out of a list of twelve on the right hand side of the detailed inspection page (conf. Figure 5.1 on page 45). When browsing through the catalog, the user has to visually search this list at every detailed inspection page to see if reviews exist for a certain document. This slows down the search process tremendously and can be found responsible for the fact that the most users are completely unaware of the existence of the service in the first hand. The best solution lies in the direct display of the reviews on the detailed inspection page. A colored graphics icon that draws the attention of the users to the link to the review page is the second best solution to heighten the visibility of a new service. Since November 2007, the link to the review page is shown in a different color (although still in the same style in the same position). The future will show, if this is enough to spread word in the potential user community about the service.

All these technical issues were known before the launch of the services. The original design of the explicit recommender system featured neither double logins nor pop-ups, but a more prominent display of reviews. This design is implemented and running within the digital library of the chair of information services and electronic markets[4] (EM) at the Universität Karlsruhe (TH). It is accessible by the staff and students of this division. The implementation and user interface design displayed in this chapter is to a large part due to the corporate design of the OPAC and the preferred web development tools (e. g. dbkit) of the Library of the Universität Karlsruhe (TH). At the choice of either staying with the much smaller user group at the EM or agreeing to interface changes and getting field experiment data from a university library, the author chose the latter. Unfortunately, user reports as well as the statistical usage analysis show that the interface changes were done in a way that highly influences the usage of the services. Chapter 9 gives a more detailed study on design issues at STI Providers.

5.5.3 Extensions

The problem of user motivation to contribute will be investigated in the future in the following form. Since the start of the services no technical incentive system like user point accounts was included, neither were any library customers directly asked to contribute. This approach was taken to measure the intrinsic motivation of customers. Next, students will be asked to write reviews on literature they are using for seminars. Thereby the number of quality reviews will be increased. The better visibility of the systems opens the way to feedback effects leading to further reviews. At a later stage it is planned to include a reputation system with lists of best reviewers, best reviews, etc. The last step would be the introduction of a compensation system to raise extrinsic motivation.

Gathering and managing metadata like keywords for all documents with a limited number of staff is a challenge for every large scientific library. Once a larger number of reviews exist, a feature to search the full text of all reviews can be used as an approximation to a user generated indexing of the library catalog. For example, typing in a course name shows literature considered useful by students (although not necessarily by the lecturer).

The ratings of reviews are a direct approach to determine the quality of a review. An alternative approach to the quality management of a review service is to bundle all reviews within a certain field in a separate review journal portal where each review undergoes the regular editorial process of such a journal. For this approach, the workflow of review-journals needs to be built around the existing review system. By

---

[4] http://www.em.uni-karlsruhe.de

means of this, new peer-reviewed review-journals can be easily set up for different scientific communities of various areas. The reviews can then be browsed either through the portal of their corresponding journal (with links to the documents within the OPAC) or directly within the OPAC at their associated documents. On the one hand, for the readers of a review, the advantage is that reviews are better integrated into the user's search process compared to traditional review-journals. On the other hand, the motivation of scientists to contribute reviews to the system is strengthened. Currently motivation to contribute mostly comes from altruism. In the future, the publication of a review which is part of an official peer-reviewed review-journal will contribute towards the author's scientific standing, thereby improving the career chances, and by means of this in the long run a better financial standing of the review author can be expected.

6

General Concepts of Behavior-Based Recommender Services

In the next chapters, the focus of this book is set on behavior-based recommender systems. In this chapter, different aspects are presented that play important roles in the general design of implicit recommendation services but do not belong to the area of mechanism design as discussed in Section 3.2. First, it is portrayed how preferences of customers can be determined from their behavior. Second, it is shown how self-selection leads to the necessary homogeneity of the user group that is used to collect the behavioral input data to the recommender system. Section 6.3 discusses different types of behavioral data and their general applicability as input data. The general knowledge discovery process of implicit recommender systems is depicted in the fourth section. Then, issues that arise when the observed users differ from the target group of the recommendation service are presented. Finally, the important service question of how many recommendations can be generated out of a certain amount of input data is discussed.

6.1 Revealed Preference Theory and Choice Sets

Paul A. Samuelson pioneered the revealed preference theory to appraise supplier options on the basis of consumer behavior [Sam38a, Sam38b, Sam48]. This theory gives the basis of how customer purchase data can be used to determine the preference structure of decision makers. Behavioral data is the best indicator of interest in a specific product and outperforms surveys with respect to reliability significantly.

Modelling the preference structure of decision makers in a classical way leads to causal models which explain the choice of the decision maker, allow prediction of future behavior and to infer actions of the seller to influence/change the choice of the decision maker (e. g. see

Kotler [Kot80]). In the setting of STI Providers causal modelling of the preference structure of decision-makers would require the identification (and estimation) of such a model which explains the choice of a decision maker or of a homogeneous group of decision makers (a customer segment) for each of the products—in the library scenario often more than 10,000,000 products. Solving the model identification problem requires selecting the subset of relevant variables out of $2^{10,000,000}$ subsets in the worst case in an optimal way. While a lot of research has investigated automatic model selection, e.g. by Theil's R^2 or Akaike's information criterion (AIC) (for further references see Maddala [Mad01, pp. 479–488]), the problem at this scale can still be considered as unsolved.

The idea to ignore interdependencies between system elements for large systems has been successfully applied in the derivation of several laws in physics. The first example is the derivation of Boltzmann's famous H-theorem where the quantity H which he defined in terms of the molecular velocity distribution function behaves exactly like the thermodynamic entropy (see Prigogine [Pri62]).

For the development of algorithms for the generation of recommendations in the next chapter the interdependencies between model variables are completely ignored. For this purpose, an ideal decision maker without preferences is constructed. Such an ideal decision maker can be regarded as a prototype of a group of homogeneous decision makers without preferences against which groups of decision makers with preferences can be tested. For a group of ideal decision makers, this is obvious, for a group of decision makers with preferences the principle of self-selection (see next section) grants homogeneity. The ideal decision maker draws k objects (each object represents a co-purchase, i.e. a product pair) out of an urn with n objects with replacement at random and—for simplicity—with equal probability. The number of possible co-purchases—and thus the event space—is unknown. In marketing several conceptual models which describe a sequence of product sets (e.g. total set $\supseteq$ awareness set $\supseteq$ consideration set $\supseteq$ choice set [Kot80, p. 153]) have been developed (see e.g. Narayana and Markin [NM75] or Spiggle and Sewall [SS87]). Narayana and Markin have investigated the size of the awareness set for several branded products empirically. For example, they report a range from 3–11 products with an average of 6.5 in the awareness set for toothpaste and similar results for other product categories. Although, as mentioned, the event space is unknown, the event space size is larger than k and in the worst case bounded by k times the maximal size of the awareness set. Considering the previously mentioned average sizes of awareness sets and the fact that the size of a market basket and thereby the number of co-purchased products k usually remains small—often $k < 20$ holds—this setup leads to sample sizes that can be handled by suited algorithms.

A survey of the statistical problems (e.g. violation of the independence of irrelevant alternatives assumption, biases in estimating choice models, etc.) related to this situation can be found in Andrews and Srinivasan [AS95] or Andrews and Manrai [AM98]. Recent advances in neuroimaging even allow experimental proofs of the influence of branding on brain activity in a choice situation which leads to models which postulate interactions between reasoning and emotional chains (e.g. Deppe et al. [DSK+05] or Bechara et al. [BDTD97]).

6.2 Self-Selection

The term self-selection is used to describe the process of individuals selecting themselves into a certain group. For an introduction on self-selection see e.g. [MR92]. James J. Heckman became famous for his investigation on self-selection as an undesirable mechanism leading to selection-bias in statistical analyses [Hec79, HS85, HS90].

In the area of recommender systems self-selection is highly welcome: it is crucial in identifying homogeneous user segments. Here, the signaling model of Michael Spence describes the utilized mechanism. Spence investigated the signaling that potential employees give employers by means of their acquisition of a certain educational degree [Spe74]. This mechanism can be translated to the signaling that customers give by purchasing or using a certain product. Behavior-based item-centered recommender services are observing the behavior of users and thereby are implicitly collecting information about the objects the users are purchasing or inspecting; the necessary homogeneity of a group of users in this case is granted by the principle of self-selection. Geyer-Schulz et al. [GSHNT03b] argue that this theory allows observation of aggregate buying processes for self-selected groups of consumers and thus the detection of outliers in aggregate processes. For a library context this is essential, because it preserves the privacy of the individual and thus addresses the problem of privacy discussed in Chapter 3.

6.3 Prices, Transaction Costs, Market Baskets, Lending Data, and Browser Sessions

Institutional flat rates via site license schemes, pay-per-view to individual customers, and fee-based digital document delivery services are the dominant pricing schemes for digital scientific and technical information today. Paper bound STI is to a large part bought by institutional libraries and then lent by the readers. The general problem that arises for behavior-based recommender systems lies in this structure: the buyers of STI products are different from the actual users. This special property of STI markets has to be taken into account when implicit recommender systems are introduced within this market. This section shows, how, by argumenting with transaction costs, the preference theory and self-selection principles can still be used to collect behavioral data within this market.

A customer segment is a set of anonymous customers with common interest shown by purchasing the same object. While a purchase in general is attributed with a certain price the customer is paying, the relevant measure is not the price but the transaction cost. The transaction cost is the complete cost incurred in making the economic exchange. While the term was coined later in the 1950s, Ronald H. Coase is famous for analyzing the concept in his influential article "The Nature of the Firm" [Coa37]. In this article he speaks of "costs of using the price mechanism". In STI markets, search costs make up a large amount of the transaction costs.

In the library environment, a purchase incidence can be identified with the closer inspection of a detailed document view recorded by the web server of the OPAC. The reason for this to work lies in the search cost which the user incurs when inspecting document details. For information products this has been shown to hold in [GSHJ02]. In this context a market basket corresponds to all detailed document views in a single user's browser session. The self-selection constraint is that the search cost of a user is so high that a user is willing only to inspect the detailed information of documents which are of interest to him. The higher the users value their time, the more effective is the self-selection constraint in this context. Inspection of the detailed information of a document signals genuine interest in the document. The self-selection constraint enforces the credibility of this signal. Furthermore, when the self-selection constraint holds, one can rely on this signal, because it will not be in the interest of users to fake interest. In addition, the self-selection constraint ensures that the recommendations are presented only to interested users since only those visit the detailed information page where recommendations are offered. Therefore, in the next chapters, a "detailed document inspection" is interpreted as a synonym to "purchase occasion" and "market baskets" as a synonym to "user sessions" within a library's OPAC.

While ordering or lending transaction data of documents are arguably closer related to purchases, for libraries often a low degree of service reduces the utility of these transaction streams for the identification of recommendations. Usage behavior can be observed at different stages: detailed inspections of documents in the OPAC, ordering paper documents from the magazine, ordering paper documents that are currently lent, and finally picking-up a paper document or downloading a file from the digital library. The main concern for the data selection is bias. It can be shown that lending and ordering data is highly biased, since e. g. students very often do not order the book they are mostly interested in, because this is already lent, but actually their consideration-set only includes documents that they will be able to obtain timely before the corresponding examination. For this reason the behavior-based recommendation service at the University Library of Karlsruhe portrayed in Chapter 8 is based on anonymized OPAC searches (hits on document inspection pages) and not on lending data.

6.4 Knowledge Discovery and Data Mining

Considering the implementation and evaluation of recommender systems, a system can be split up into different processes with evaluation aspects from different research fields. Generally, recommender systems fall into the field of KDD, sometimes used as an abbreviation of "Knowledge Discovery in Databases" and sometimes of "Knowledge Discovery and Data mining". Figure 6.1 displays the internal processes of an implicit recommender system in a linear way. The first three sections of this chapter have dealt with the selection of the data. The preprocessing step is described within the next case study in Section 8.1.1. The algorithms for the data mining process and their interpretation are described in general form in Chapter 7 and more specific in Chapter 8 for the case of the University Library of Karlsruhe. The presentation process is discussed by means of human computer interface design in Chapter 9. The utility evaluation of a recommender system needs to consider all processes.

6.5 Observed Users vs. Target Group of Recommendations

One of the main mechanism design problems of behavior-based recommender systems is the cold start problem (conf. Section 3.2). A certain

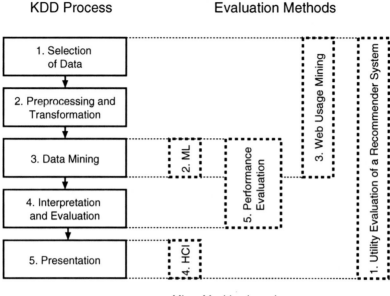

ML ... Machine Learning,
HCI ... Human Computer Interface Design

Fig. 6.1. KDD processes of an implicit recommender system

amount of usage data has to be observed before the first recommendations can be computed. To overcome this problem, sometimes usage data from different but similar applications is used to lessen the cold start problem. But starting with recommendations drawn from almost similar applications in general is a bad idea since it can not be guaranteed that the usage patterns of customers in these applications are identical. This holds for explicit systems as well as has been discussed in Section 4.4.2. Behavior-based recommendations are best suited to the user group whose usage data is used to generate the very same recommendations. The group of observed users should ideally be identical with the target group of the recommendations. Thus, to lessen the cold start problem it is better to use small sample test statistics to faster generate quality recommendations out of the first small samples of user behavior as portrayed in Section 7.2.

6.6 Factors for the Diffusion of Recommendations

When one suggests the introduction of behavior-based recommender systems to STI providers, inevitably the question arises: how many product recommendations does such a system generate? In e-commerce obviously holds: the more the better (conf. the analysis of Amazon.com in Section 4.3). From the scientific point of view it is clear that generally, considering the same input data, the quantity of generated recommendations is negatively correlated to the quality of these recommendations. While the quantity and quality highly depend on the used algorithm, some general factors for the diffusion of item-centered recommendations out of the noise of the market basket input data can be determined.

The amount of new recommendations by time in item-centered behavior-based systems is influenced by the following factors:

The total amount of available usage data. Generally   speaking, the more data the better.

The number of products. When leaving the amount of usage data fixed, the larger the number of used products, the longer it generally takes for a single product to get significantly many purchases for statistical recommendation analysis.

The size of the market baskets. With a fixed amount of single purchases, fewer but larger market baskets contain more co-purchases than many small baskets.

The usage distribution of the products. With a uniform product usage distribution it takes longer for recommendations to appear than with highly skewed distributions. In the latter case, some products are bought much more often than others, these highly frequented products will have recommendations before the less frequented ones. Because of this recommendations are generated for the used part of a library early.

7

Algorithms for Behavior-Based Recommender Systems

Different methodologies exist for the generation of behavior-based recommendations. This chapter focuses on methods that are especially suited to the needs and challenges associated with the application area of STI providers. The behavioral input data consists of market baskets that can be found likewise in e-commerce, library environments, or (Web 2.0) social network sites. The relevant problem that has to be solved is the question, which co-purchases or co-inspections of products in the market baskets occur non-randomly thus hinting at an underlying relation of these products. First, a method developed for large samples based on calculating inspection frequency distribution functions following a logarithmic series distribution is presented. Second, two algorithms for small samples—to ease the cold start problem of new recommendation services—are described. Third, a short overview of related methods including a comparison with the previously presented methods is given.

7.1 Purchase Noise Filtering by Means of the Logarithmic Series Distribution

The algorithm presented in this section aggregates the market basket data into inspection frequency distribution functions to generate recommendations. The method is based on Ehrenberg's repeat-buying theory [Ehr88]. Recommendation services operational at different information providers that rely on this method are presented in Chapter 8. The description of the algorithm in this section is based on [GSHNT03b].

This section is structured as follows: in Section 7.1.1 a general introduction into Ehrenberg's ideas is given, Section 7.1.2 presents the classical repeat-buying theory for consumer panel analysis, Section 7.1.3

describes the modifications necessary to make this theory applicable to anonymous market basket data, and finally, the algorithm for the generation of recommendations is presented in Section 7.1.4.

7.1.1 Ehrenberg's Repeat-Buying Theory

In purchasing a non-durable consumer product a consumer basically makes two decisions: the decision to purchase a product of a certain product class (purchase incidence) and the decision to choose a certain brand (brand choice). Ehrenberg's main conceptual insight is that repeat-buying behavior can be adequately modeled by formalizing the purchase incidence process of a single brand. As a result Ehrenberg's repeat-buying theory is of a considerable simplicity and elegance:

> *Of the thousand and one variables which might affect buyer behavior, it is found that nine hundred and ninety-nine usually do not matter. Many aspects of buyer behavior can be predicted simply from the penetration and the average purchase frequency of an item, and even these two variables are interrelated.*
>
> A. S. C. Ehrenberg [Ehr88]

Historically, repeat-buying theory was developed for the analysis of consumer panels. A consumer panel consists of a sample of consumers who report their purchases completely and faithfully to a marketing research company like e. g. ACNielsen. Such a full report contains the sequence of all purchases of a consumer over an extensive period of time for all outlets and is called the purchase history of a consumer. The list of products purchased at a single trip to the store is called a market basket. In a consumer panel the identity of each consumer is known and an individual purchase history can be constructed from the union of all market baskets of a single consumer. Crucial for the success of consumer panel analysis was the choice of purchase occasions as unit of analysis. A purchase occasion is a binary variable coded as one if a consumer has purchased at least one item of a product in a trip to a store and zero otherwise. The number of items purchased as well as package sizes are ignored. One of the earliest uses of purchase occasions can be attributed to L. J. Rothman [S.R65].

Ehrenberg's classic book [Ehr88] on repeat-buying theory remains a readable standard reference and a suitable introduction to consumer panel analysis for the practitioner. The theory presented in the next section can be found in much more detail there. However, in order to be applicable for recommender systems the following insight, which is not at the center of Ehrenberg's theory, is necessary. Ehrenberg's theory faithfully models the noise part of buying processes. That is, repeat-buying theory is capable of predicting random co-purchases of consumer goods. Intentionally bought combinations of consumer goods as e. g. a six-pack of beer, spare-ribs, potatoes, and barbecue-sauce for dinner are outliers. In this sense, Ehrenberg's theory acts as a filter to suppress noise (stochastic regularity) in buying behavior.

7.1.2 Repeat-Buying Theory for Consumer Panel Analysis

Consumer panel analysis is carried out in distinct time-periods (such as 1-week, 4-week, quarterly periods) conforming with other standard marketing reporting practices. A particular simplification resulting from this time-period orientation is that most repeat-buying results for any given item can be expressed in terms of penetration and purchase frequency. The penetration is the proportion of consumers who buy an item at all within a given period. The purchase frequency w is the average number of times these consumers buy at least one item in the period. The mean purchase frequency w is itself the most basic measure of repeat-buying in Ehrenberg's theory and in this book.

By arguing that consumers purchase products independently, because of e. g. restocking items only as necessary, Ehrenberg [Ehr88, p. 128] postulated the following stochastic process model of compound Poisson form for the description of stationary purchasing behavior over a sequence of equal periods of time:

1. Purchases of a specific consumer are regarded as independent drawings from a Poisson distribution.
2. The average purchase rates of consumers differ in the long run, they follow a Gamma-distribution with exponent k and mean m.

These assumptions lead directly to a negative binomial distribution (NBD) with exponent k and mean $m = ak$ for the probability of observing a consumer with r purchase occurrences in the observation period:

$$P_r = \int_0^\infty \frac{e^{-\frac{\mu}{a}}\mu^{k-1}}{a^k \Gamma(k)} \frac{e^{-\mu}\mu^r}{r!} d\mu = (1+a)^{-k} \frac{\Gamma(k+r)}{\Gamma(r+1)\Gamma(k)} \left(\frac{a}{1+a}\right)^r \quad (7.1)$$

with variance $\sigma^2 = m\left(1 + \frac{m}{k}\right)$.

In day-to-day marketing practice this theory successfully predicts, which proportion of buyers of a product buy it also in the next period and which not, how often repeat-buyers buy in each period, and

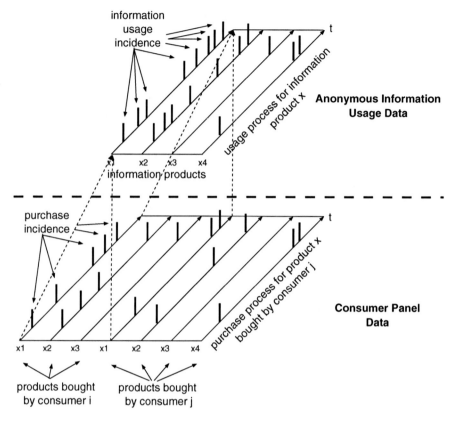

Fig. 7.1. Adapting consumer panel purchase incidences to anonymous information usage data

what the influence of light, medium, and heavy buyers is on the purchases of the next period. In addition, Ehrenberg suggests that this model with its strong independence structure explains the regularities in markets and thus can be used as a filter to discover non-random deviations from regular market behavior. It is this last usage which will be exploited here by using repeat-buying theory to account for random co-occurrences of products and thus to identify deviations as interesting recommendations.

The lower level of Figure 7.1 illustrates the basic idea of Ehrenberg's purchase incidence models: a consumer in a panel purchases a specific consumer product following a stationary Poisson process. This process is independent of the other purchase processes of the consumer. The rationale is that in each household certain consumer products are stored and only restocked as soon as the household runs out of the item

(e. g. coffee, soap, tooth-paste). Chatfield et al. [CEG66] proved that aggregating these purchase processes over a population of consumers under the (quite general) assumption that the parameters μ of the Poisson distributions of the purchase processes of the individual consumers (the long run average purchase rates) follow a truncated Γ-distribution results in a logarithmic series distribution (LSD).

The LSD is a one parameter (q) distribution which gives according to Ehrenberg the probability that a specific product is purchased a total of 1, 2, 3, ..., r times without knowing the number of non-buyers. Its frequency distribution $P(r$ purchases$)$, its mean w (the mean purchase frequency), and its variance σ^2 are shown in Formulas 7.2, 7.3, and 7.4, respectively. Note that $\sigma^2 > w$ is a characteristic of the LSD distribution. For further details on the LSD distribution, see e. g. [JKK93].

$$P(r \text{ purchases}) = \frac{-q^r}{r \ln(1-q)}, \quad r \geq 1 \tag{7.2}$$

$$w = \frac{-q}{(1-q)\ln(1-q)} \tag{7.3}$$

$$\sigma^2 = \frac{w}{(1-q)} - w^2 = \frac{-q\left(1 + \frac{q}{\ln(1-q)}\right)}{(1-q)^2 \ln(1-q)} \tag{7.4}$$

The following assumptions on consumer purchase behavior lead to a LSD:

1. The share of never-buyers in the population is unknown. In the classic consumer panel setting, this assumption is usually unnecessary. However, in Internet environments, this assumption definitely holds and is necessary. The implication of this is that it restricts the analysis to the LSD-model which in consumer panel analysis serves only as an approximation for the negative binomial distribution (NBD) model.

2. The purchases of a consumer in successive periods is Poisson distributed with an average μ which can be observed in the long run if a purchase is independent of previous purchases (as is often observed) and a purchase occurs in an irregular manner that seems random (see [WT87] for more details).

3. The distribution of μ in the population follows a truncated Γ-distribution so that the frequency of any particular value of μ is given by $(ce^{-\mu/a}/\mu)d\mu$, for $\delta \leq \mu \leq \infty$, where δ is a very small number, a a parameter of the distribution, and c a constant so that $\int_\delta^\infty (ce^{-\mu/a}/\mu)d\mu = 1$.

Ehrenberg's argument [Ehr88, p. 259] for a Γ-distribution of the μ in the population of consumer purchase processes is the following: if for different products $x_1, x_2, x_3, x_4, \ldots$ the average purchase rate of x_1 is independent of the purchase rates of the other products, and $\frac{x_1}{(x_1+x_2+x_3+x_4+\ldots)}$ is independent of a consumer's total purchase rate of buying all the products then it can be shown that the distribution of μ must be a Γ-distribution. In several consumer panel studies these independence conditions have been shown to hold at least approximately (for example see [Ask75, CE76, PW78, Sic82]).

4. The market is stationary or in equilibrium. This is violated e. g., when new brands in a consumer product market are launched. For STI providers, new acquisitions of books is an example for the violation of this assumption. Still, as long as new acquisitions constitute only a tiny fraction when compared to the full collection, we assume that this condition still tends to hold for most documents most of the time.

That these assumptions lead indeed to an LSD distribution can be seen from Chatfield's proof whose most important steps are repeated here for the sake of completeness:

1. The probability p_r of r purchases of a consumer is $\frac{e^{-\mu}\mu^r}{r!}$ (Poisson).
2. Integration over all consumers in the truncated Γ-distribution leads to

$$p_r = c \int_\delta^\infty \frac{e^{-\mu}\mu^r}{r!} \frac{e^{-\frac{\mu}{a}}}{\mu} d\mu$$

$$= \frac{c}{r!(1+\frac{1}{a})^r} \int_\delta^\infty e^{-(1+\frac{1}{a})\mu}((1+\frac{1}{a})\mu)^{r-1} d(1+\frac{1}{a})\mu \quad (7.5)$$

Let $r \geq 1$, $t = (1+1/a)\mu$, and $q = \frac{a}{1+a}$. Since δ is very small, one can approximate

$$p_r = \frac{c}{r!(1+\frac{1}{a})^r} \int_\delta^\infty e^{-t} t^{r-1} dt$$

$$\approx \frac{c}{r!(1+\frac{1}{a})^r} \Gamma(r) = c\frac{q^r}{r} = q p_{r-1}(r-1)/r \quad (7.6)$$

3. For $r \geq 1$, $\sum p_r = 1$ holds. Therefore, by analyzing the recursion $p_1 = \frac{-q}{\ln(1-q)}$ and $p_r = \frac{-q^r}{r \ln(1-q)}$ hold. (Compare with Formula 7.2.)

7.1.3 Repeat-Buying Theory for Anonymous Market Basket Data

So far about repeat-buying theory in the classic marketing setting of consumer panel analysis. A direct application of this theory in the context of STI providers, especially scientific libraries, immediately evokes the following seemingly obvious counter-arguments:

- Users hardly ever borrow a book more than once. So, there are almost no repeat-buys in the data.
- Per document payment for the service is rare to non-existent (see [Neu07c] both for the general statement and counterexamples).
- Ehrenberg's repeat-buying theory is based on purchase histories. The classic model presented in Section 7.1.2 can not be applied to anonymous session data which is the only data source that can be analyzed at public institutions like libraries under the privacy requirements of data protection laws (in Germany the Datenschutzgesetz).
- Ehrenberg's repeat-buying theory is for homogeneous and stationary markets only. A STI provider usually serves a heterogeneous, even fragmented market with non-stationarities in important market segments (e. g. information technology).

Nevertheless, the following will show that these arguments do not hold. The general similarity of market baskets, browser sessions, and library lending data has already been discussed in Section 6.3. For the STI setting the upper level of Figure 7.1 is considered. The basic idea is to treat anonymous market baskets as a consumer panel with unobserved consumer identity. This implies that the purchase process of a document which can be observed is an aggregation of all purchase processes of all users of the library which inspect a certain detailed document view. In Figure 7.1 this aggregation process is illustrated for document x_1 by the dotted arrows from the lower to the upper level. In consumer panel analysis such aggregations have not been of interest yet. However, e. g. for planning the capacity of local nodes of a telephone system similar aggregate processes (of incoming calls) are traditionally modelled as Poisson-processes for the analysis as queuing systems.

Although penetration is easily measured within personalized systems, here penetration is of less concern, because in the library setting the proportion of library users in the population is unknown due to the anonymity of market baskets.

For giving recommendations, document pairs have to be considered. That is for some fixed document x in the set X of documents of the library the purchase frequency of pairs of (x, i) with $i \in X \setminus x$. The probability $p_r(x \wedge i)$ that users make r inspections of detailed document views x and i during the same sessions which follow independent Poisson processes with means μ_x and μ_i is [JKB97]: $p_r(x \wedge i) = \frac{e^{-\mu_x}\mu_x^r}{r!}\frac{e^{-\mu_i}\mu_i^r}{r!}$. For the recommendations for document x, the conditional probability, that document i has been inspected under the condition that document x has been inspected in the same session, is needed. Because of the independence assumption it is easy to see [GSHJ02] that the conditional probability $p_r(i \mid x)$ is again Poisson distributed by

$$p_r(i \mid x) = \frac{p_r(x \wedge i)}{p_r(x)} = \frac{\frac{e^{-\mu_x}\mu_x^r}{r!}\frac{e^{-\mu_i}\mu_i^r}{r!}}{\frac{e^{-\mu_x}\mu_x^r}{r!}} = \frac{e^{-\mu_i}\mu_i^r}{r!} = p_r(i). \qquad (7.7)$$

With the help of self-selection, purchase processes for each library user segment—a set of anonymous users with common interests which inspected a document pair in the same session respectively—can be identified. The occurrence of repeat-purchases in a library setting on the aggregate level is best explained by the way research is done at a university. Today research is organized as a communication-intensive team-effort including university teachers and students. Repeat purchases on the aggregate level are now triggered by several informal word-of-mouth processes like e. g. the tutoring of students in a seminar or the recommendations given in various feedback and review processes. A second effect which triggers repeat-purchases is the complementary nature of the net of science: e. g. several independent application-oriented research groups in marketing research, telecommunications, statistics, and operations research apply Poisson-processes in their field of study. For each of these segments the purchase histories can be identified as follows [GSHJ02]: For each document x the purchase history for this segment contains all sessions in which x has been inspected. For each pair of documents (x, i) the purchase history for this segment contains all sessions in which (x, i) has been inspected. The stochastic process for the (x, i) segment—n library users which have inspected document x and another document i—is represented by the sum of n independent random Bernoulli variables which equal 1 with probability p_i, and 0 with probability $1 - p_i$. The distribution of the sum of these variables tends to a Poisson distribution. For a proof see Feller [Fel71, p. 292]. Assuming that the parameters μ of the segments' Poisson distributions follow a truncated Γ-distribution, Chatfield's proof can be repeated and thus establishes that the probability of r inspections of document pairs (x, i) follow a LSD.

However, it is expected that non-random occurrences of such pairs occur more often than predicted by the logarithmic series distribution because of the way research and teaching is organized at a research university and that non-random occurrences of such pairs can be identified and used as recommendations. For this purpose the LSD for the whole market (over all consumers) from market baskets is estimated from anonymous web-sessions. The mean purchase frequency w is computed and Equation 7.3 is solved for q, the parameter of the LSD. By comparing the observed repeat-buying frequencies with the theoretically expected frequencies outliers are identified as recommendations.

The LSD-model limits the kind of market analysis that can be conducted. For example, analysis of the behavior of different types of library users (e. g. light and heavy users) is possible only with a full NBD-model.

A recommendation for a document x simply is an outlier of the LSD-model, i. e. a document y that has been used more often in the same session as could have been expected from independent random choice acts. A recommendation reveals a complementarity between documents.

The main purpose of the LSD-model in this setting is to separate non-random co-occurrences of information products (outliers) from random co-occurrences (as expected from the LSD-model). The LSD-model is used as a filter for discovering irregularities.

7.1.4 The LSD-Algorithm for the Generation of Recommendations

Table 7.1 presents the algorithm that is derived from the theory of the previous sections. As necessary in repeat-buying theory step 1 of the algorithm counts repeated usage of two information products in a single session only once. A rationale for this correction is that repeated inspection of detailed meta data for documents in a single session reflects the user's decision process leading to a purchase decision. Step 2 of the algorithm discards all frequency distributions with a small number of observations. The reason is that no valid LSD-model can be estimated. Of course, the implication is that for these cases no recommendations are given; Section 7.2 presents solutions how to compute recommendations for these cases. For each remaining frequency distribution, step 3 computes the mean purchase frequency, the LSD parameter, and the outliers as recommendations.

Table 7.1. The LSD-algorithm for the generation of recommendations

1. Compute for all documents x in the market baskets the frequency distributions $f(x_{obs})$ for repeat-purchases of the co-occurrences of x with other documents in a session, i. e. of the pair (x, i) with $i \in X \setminus x$. Several co-occurrences of a pair (x, i) in a single session are counted only once. (Frequency distribution)
2. Discard all frequency distributions with less than l observations. (Current setting: $l = 10$)
3. For each frequency distribution:
    a) Compute the robust mean purchase frequency w by trimming the sample by removing x percent of the high repeat-buy pairs. (Current setting: $x = 20\%$)
    b) Estimate the parameter q for the LSD-model from
       $w = \frac{-q}{(1-q)(\ln(1-q))}$
       (Currently by a bisection method)
    c) Apply a χ^2-goodness-of-fit test with a suitable α between the observed and the expected LSD distribution $f(x_{exp})$ with a suitable partitioning. (Current settings: 0.01 and 0.05)
    d) Determine the outliers in the tail. Compute for each r of repeat-buys the ratio s_r of the observed frequency to the expected frequency according to the LSD-model: $s_r = \frac{f_r(x_{exp})}{f_r(x_{obs})}$.
       If $s_r < t$ with t a suitable threshold, then all documents in class r are recommended. (Current setting: $t = 0.5$)

High repeat-buy outliers may have a considerable impact on the mean purchase frequency and thus on the parameter of the distribution. The statistical standard procedure for outliers is trimming the sample (step 3a). By computing a robust mean the chances of finding a significant LSD-model are considerably improved.

In step 3d outliers are identified as belonging to classes with r repeat-buys if the ratio of the expected random co-occurrences according to the LSD-model to the observed co-occurrences is below a certain threshold. The threshold can be interpreted as the maximum acceptable percentage of random co-occurrences recommended. Several other options for determining the outliers in the tail of the distribution are possible:

1. Outliers at r are above $\sum_r^\infty f_r(x_{exp})$.
2. Set β as the acceptable type two error for recommendations, i. e. recommending a document although it is only a random co-occurrence.

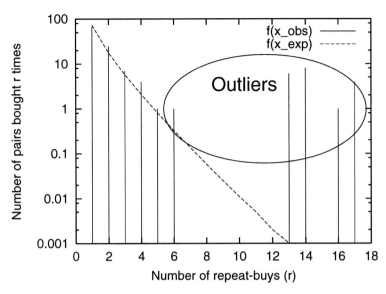

Fig. 7.2. Exemplary logarithmic plot of the observed and expected (LSD) inspection frequency distribution

Accept all documents in classes $r \ldots \infty$ with $\sum_r^\infty f_r(x_{exp}) < \beta$. From the boundary class $r + 1$ draw j documents at random (anyway you like) as long as $\beta - \sum_r^\infty f_r(x_{exp}) > j \cdot \frac{f_{r+1}(x_{exp})}{n \cdot f_{r+1}(x_{obs})}$.

These options lead to variants of the method which exhibit different first and second type errors.

As Figure 7.2 here exemplarily shows, the framework described above holds for STI providers, in this case for the book "Infrared and Raman Spectroscopy" by Bernhard Schrader (1995) in the UBKA. The observed frequency distribution $f(x \text{ obs})$ corresponds to the ranking by decreasing number of repeated co-purchases in the list of recommendations presented to the user. An example of the user interface of this list will be given in the case study on behavior-based recommendation services presented in Chapter 8 (see Figure 8.4 on page 96). Recommendations are the outliers, i.e. products that have been bought together more often than expected by the stochastic model. More specifically, an LSD-model with a robust mean of 1.410 and a robust parameter $q = 0.479$ passes a χ^2-goodness-of-fit test at $\alpha = 0.01$ ($\chi^2 = 8.016$ which is below 13.816, the critical value at $\alpha = 0.01$). Table 7.2 shows the corresponding statistical output of the LSD-algorithm. More detailed statistics for the generation of a complete set of recommendations are provided in the case study on behavior-based recommendation services presented in Chapter 8 (see Table 8.4 on page 107).

7.2 POSICI and POMICI: Recommendations from Small Samples

In Section 3.2 the cold start problem was determined as one of the key problems with the introduction of new recommendation services. Although, as stated there, it is of less concern with behavior-based services and even more so in the case of value-added services connected to already existing websites with regular user traffic, it is commonly of main concern to the system operator that the new service becomes visible and helpful to the users as fast as possible. In this section two algorithms, first published by Neumann and Geyer-Schulz in [NGS08], are described that were developed to generate recommendations out of small samples of co-purchases of products. They speed up the diffusion of recommendations especially at an early stage of a new introduced service—for a faster return on investment of recommender projects—or for products recently added to the catalog. The application area lies within sample sizes of co-purchase frequencies that do not allow a more sophisticated statistical analysis like the LSD-approach presented in Section 7.1. The cold start problem is lessened by faster generating quality recommendations out of the first small samples of user behavior. Nevertheless, the critical point remains to reliably separate meaningful co-purchases from random ones.

The development was motivated by a case study in one of the possible application areas: German library meta catalogs. An analysis of market basket sizes at different organizational levels of German research library networks revealed that at the highest network level market basket size is considerably smaller than at the university level, thus leading to less co-purchases (conf. to Section 6.6). In analogy to the LSD-approach of Section 7.1 the independent stochastic processes are modelled. The co-purchase frequencies with a high occurrence probability are considered as noise and the unlikely ones are the basis for the generation of recommendations. The statistical tests are based on modelling the choice-acts of a decision maker completely without preferences as described in Section 6.1.

Table 7.2. Example of the statistical output of the LSD-algorithm

```
Web-site: 4122050§UBKA_OPAC
Total number of observations: 124
Max repeat-buys: 17
Sample mean=3.5241935483871 and var=22.5236082206035
Case: E var>mean
Estimate for q=0.883334725189209

Robust estimation: Trimmed begin 0: 0 / end 0.2: 24 (24 observations)
Robust estimation: Number of observations: 100
Robust mean=1.41 and var=0.4019
Robust estimate for q=0.478939454650879

Plot: Observed repeat-buys and robust estimated LSD
      (q=0.478939454650879)
repeat-buys  nf(x_obs)  nf(x_exp)  f(x_exp)/f(x_obs)  show
          1         67     73.469              1.097     0
          2         25     17.594              0.704     0
          3          8      5.618              0.702     0
          4          4      2.018              0.504     0
          5          0      0.773                  -     0
          6          1      0.309              0.309     1
          7          0      0.127                  -     0
          8          0      0.053                  -     0
          9          0      0.023                  -     0
         10          0      0.010                  -     0
         11          0      0.004                  -     0
         12          0      0.002                  -     0
         13          6      0.001              0.000     1
         14          8      0.000              0.000     1
         15          0      0.000                  -     0
         16          1      0.000              0.000     1
         17          4      0.000              0.000     1
Recommendations found with threshold=0.5:  20

Chi-square test for q=0.883334725189209 and 124 observations
Class  nf(x_obs)  nf(x_exp)  chi-square
    1         67     50.983       5.032
    2         25     22.517       0.274
    3          8     13.260       2.087
    4          4      8.785       2.606
    5          0      6.208       6.208
    6         20     22.247       0.227
                            ------------
                                 16.434
```

Table 7.2. (continued)

```
Chi-square test for q=0.478939454650879 and 100 observations
Class  nf(x_obs)  nf(x_exp)   chi-square
   1       67       73.469       0.570
   2       25       17.594       3.117
   3        8        5.618       1.010
   4        0        3.319       3.319
                              ------------
                                 8.016

Robust estimate performes better with chi-square value: 8.016
Chi-square test threshold with alpha=0.05 and 2 d.f.:5.991
Chi-square test threshold with alpha=0.01 and 2 d.f.:13.816
Sample comes from LSD with alpha=0.01
Col: IV
```

Table 7.3. Statistical properties of the data (status of 2007-02-19)

	UBKA	KVK
Number of total documents in catalog	$\sim 1{,}000{,}000$	$> 10{,}000{,}000$
Number of total co-inspected documents	527,363	255,248
Average market basket size	4.9	2.9
Av. aggregated co-inspections per document	117.4	5.4

7.2.1 A Motivational Example: Statistical Properties of Market Baskets in Library Meta Catalogs

Table 7.3 shows some characteristics of the usage data of the UBKA and Karlsruhe's Virtual Catalog (KVK)[1], a meta library catalog searching 52 international catalogs. Because of the smaller market basket size, the shorter observation period, and the much higher (unknown) number of total documents in the meta catalog KVK, the average aggregated co-inspections per document in the KVK is very small. The distribution for $k \leq 15$ is shown in Figure 7.3. Due to sample size constraints methods using statistical tests on distributions (like LSD) are only reliably applicable with many co-inspections. Special small sample statistics are needed to compute recommendations out of samples of few co-inspections. POSICI and POMICI are based on the assumption that all documents in the catalog have the same probability of being co-inspected. In real systems generally this assumption does not hold, but especially when starting to observe new catalogs no information about the underlying distribution of the inspection processes of documents is

---

[1] http://kvk.ubka.uni-karlsruhe.de

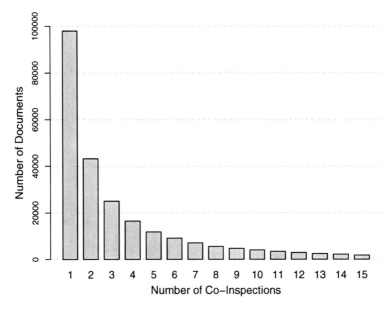

Fig. 7.3. Distribution of co-inspections in the KVK for $k \leq 15$ (status of 2007-02-19)

known. Finally, recommendations are co-inspections that occur significantly more often then predicted in the case of the assumption being true.

7.2.2 Mathematical Setup

For the mathematical formulation the following notation is used. The number of total documents $n + 1$ in the catalog is finite but unknown (this leaves n documents as possible co-inspections for each document D in the catalog). Recommendations are computed separately for each document D. Each user session (market basket) contains all documents that the user inspected within that session, multiple inspections of the same document are counted as one. All user sessions are aggregated. The aggregated set $C(D)$ contains all documents that at least one user has inspected together with D. The number of co-inspections with D of all elements of $C(D)$ is known, this histogram is called $H(D)$, it is the outcome of a multinomial experiment. When removing all documents with no inspections from $H(D)$ and then re-writing the number of co-inspections as a sum, it can be interpreted as an integer partition of k with the number of co-inspections of each co-inspected document as the

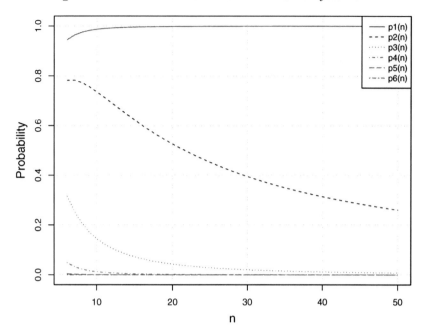

Fig. 7.4. Inspection probabilities $p_j\,(n)$ for $k = 6$ and $n = 6, \ldots, 50$ in POSICI

addends. k is the number of non-aggregated co-inspections (multiple inspections in different sessions are counted separately). For the theory of partitions see Andrews [And76].

For example, $4+1+1$ is an integer partition of $k = 6$ and shows that the corresponding document D has been co-inspected in at least 4 (the highest number) different sessions with 3 (the number of addends) other documents, with the first document 4 times and with the second and third one time each. Two different options for the computation of recommendations are considered. Taking the addends as input separately leads to the POSICI algorithm; taking the partition as a whole leads to the POMICI algorithm. Algorithm input: $\begin{cases} [4],[1] & \Rightarrow \text{POSICI.} \\ [4+1+1] & \Rightarrow \text{POMICI.} \end{cases}$

7.2.3 POSICI: Probability of Single Item Co-Inspections

The first method presented here is based on the following question:

> What is the probability $p_j\,(n)$ that at least one other document has been co-inspected exactly j times with document D?

To answer the question the setup of the multinomial distribution is used directly. Let $(N_1, \ldots, N_n)$ be the vector of the number of times

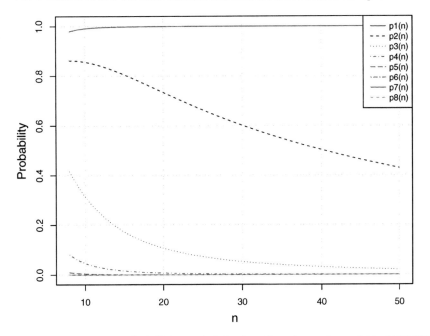

Fig. 7.5. Inspection probabilities $p_j(n)$ for $k = 8$ and $n = 8\ldots, 50$ in POSICI

document i ($1 \leq i \leq n$) was co-inspected with D. Then $(N_1, \ldots, N_n) \sim \mathcal{M}(k; q_1, \ldots, q_n)$, $q_i = \frac{1}{n}$, $1 \leq i \leq n$. Now define $A_i = \{N_i = j\}$. By applying the inclusion-exclusion principle one can now compute:

$$p_j(n) = P\left(\bigcup_{i=1}^{n} A_i\right) = \sum_{\nu=1}^{n} (-1)^{\nu-1} \sum_{1 \leq i_1 < \ldots < i_\nu \leq n} P(A_{i_1} \cap \ldots \cap A_{i_\nu})$$

(7.8)

Since many of the addends on the right hand side are known to be equal to zero, this equation can be implemented quite efficiently. Figure 7.4 shows $p_j(n)$ for $k = 6$ and growing n and Figure 7.5 displays the distribution of the probabilities for $k = 8$. In general $\lim_{n \to \infty} p_1(n) = 1$ and $\lim_{n \to \infty} p_j(n) = 0$ for $j = 2, 3, \ldots$ holds. Further on, $p_j(n)$ is decreasing in j for all n. Based on these probabilities the computation of recommendations is defined by the following algorithm.

POSICI Recommendation Generating Algorithm:

1. Let D be the document for which recommendations are calculated.
2. Let $n = k$ and t be a fixed chosen acceptance threshold ($0 < t < 1$).
3. Determine $j_0 = \min_{j=2,\ldots,k} \{j \mid p_j(n) < t\, p_1(n)\}$.

4. Recommend all documents that have been co-inspected with D at least j_0 times.

Thus, e. g. in the setting of Figure 7.5 and $t = 0.2$ all documents that have been co-inspected at least 4 times are being recommended. POSICI is built on the theory that co-inspections other than j times add more noise than information about the incentive to co-inspect the current document j times.

7.2.4 POMICI: Probability of Multiple Items Co-Inspections

The second method is derived from the question:

> What is the probability $p_{part}(n)$ that the partition corresponding to the complete histogram $H(D)$ of all co-inspections with D occurs?

To answer this question the problem is re-formulated in an algebraic setting. Let X be the set of words of length k from an alphabet of n letters, and l_i the number of letters (i. e. documents) that occur exactly i times in $x \in X$ (i. e. in $H(D)$). Two groups are acting on the set X:

- The symmetric group S_n of all permutations of the n letters
- The symmetric group S_k of all permutations of the k positions of a word

The actions of the groups S_n and S_k commute thus inducing the action of the group $G := S_n \times S_k$ on X.

Definition 7.1. *Let $x \in X$. The subset $Gx := \{gx \mid g \in G\}$ of X is called the **orbit** of x under the action of G.*

To answer the previous stated question, the cardinality of the orbits of the action of G on X has to be determined to compute

$$p_{part}(n) = \frac{|Gx|}{|X|} \tag{7.9}$$

Since this can not be done in a straight-forward way, some more theory is necessary.

Definition 7.2. *Let $x \in X$. The subgroup $G_x := \{g \in G \mid gx = x\}$ of G is called the **stabilizer** of x under the action of G.*

The following theorem now helps with the computation of the cardinalities.

Theorem 7.3. *Orbit-stabilizer theorem. With the above definitions,*
$|G| = |Gx| |G_x|$ *holds.*

The cardinality of X and the order of G are easily determined:

$$|X| = n^k, \quad |G| = |S_n| |S_k| = n! \, k! \qquad (7.10)$$

By means of the orbit-stabilizer theorem, Equation 7.9 can now be written in the form:

$$p_{part}(n) = \frac{|Gx|}{|X|} = \frac{|G|}{|X| |G_x|} \qquad (7.11)$$

$|G_x|$ is still unknown. To compute it, the orbit-stabilizer theorem is applied a second time. Now, the orbit of the identity element id of the action of the group G_x on the set S_n is considered. The resulting equality is frequently stated in the literature as a corollary to Lagrange's group theorem:

$$|G_x| = |G_x id| \, |G_{x id}| \qquad (7.12)$$

Remember l_i to be the number of the kinds of letters that appear exactly i times within the word x. Then, the orbit $G_x id$ is isomorphic to $\times_{i=0}^{k} S_{l_i}$, since only letters in a word can be permuted that appear in the same amount and every permutation of this kind can be realized by one element of G_x. Thus, the following holds:

$$|G_x id| = |\bigtimes_{i=0}^{k} S_{l_i}| = \left(n - \sum_{i=1}^{k} l_i\right)! \prod_{j=1}^{k} l_j! \qquad (7.13)$$

The stabilizer group $G_{x id}$ is composed of those pairs $(id, g) \in G$, of which the permutation g of the k positions leaves the word x invariant. $(j!)^{l_j}$ is the number of the permutations of those letters that can be found j times within the word x. Thus, the order of the stabilizer can be computed to be:

$$|G_{x id}| = \prod_{j=1}^{k} (j!)^{l_j} \qquad (7.14)$$

By putting all previous results together, the question at the beginning of this section can be answered. The probability $p_{part}(n)$, that the partition corresponding to the complete histogram $H(D)$ of all co-inspections with D occurs, can be calculated to be:

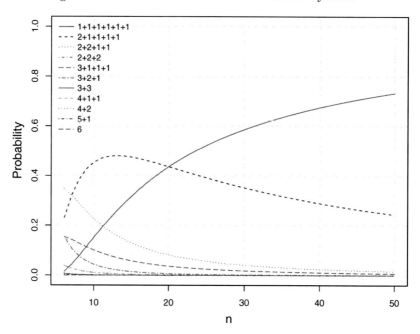

Fig. 7.6. Inspection probabilities $p_{part}(n)$ for $k = 6$ and $n = 6, \ldots, 50$ in POMICI

$$p_{part}(n) = \frac{|Gx|}{|X|} = \frac{|G|}{|X|\,|G_x id|\,|G_{x id}|}$$

$$= \frac{n!\,k!}{n^k \left(n - \sum_{i=1}^{k} l_i\right)! \prod_{j=1}^{k} l_j!\,(j!)^{l_j}} \qquad (7.15)$$

In general $\lim_{n \to \infty} p_{1 + \cdots + 1}(n) = 1$ and $= 0$ for all other partitions holds. As can be seen exemplary in Figures 7.6 and 7.7, depending on k only above a certain n the order by probability of the partitions is stable. The smallest of these n is used for the computation of recommendations.

POMICI Recommendation Generating Algorithm:

1. Let D be the document for which recommendations are calculated.
2. Let t be a fixed chosen acceptance threshold $(0 < t < 1)$.
3. Let n_D be the smallest integer, after which the order by probability of the partitions for $n \geq n_D$ is stable.
4. Let s be the largest integer that occurs in the partition with the highest probability below $t\,p_{1 + \cdots + 1}(n_D)$.

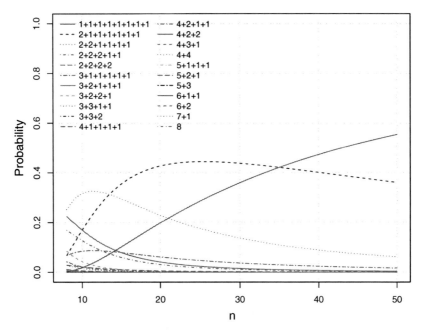

Fig. 7.7. Inspection probabilities $p_{part}(n)$ for $k = 8$ and $n = 8, \ldots, 50$ in POMICI

5. For all partitions *part* with $p_{part}(n_D) < t\, p_{1+\cdots+1}(n_D)$ do
   a) Recommend all documents from $H(D)$ that have been co-inspected at least s times.

Thus, e. g. in the setting of Figure 7.6 and $t = 0.05$ all documents that have been observed within the partitions $3 + 2 + 1$, $3 + 3$, $4 + 1 + 1$, $4 + 2$, $5 + 1$ or 6 and have been co-inspected at least 3 times are being recommended ($n_D = 21$, $p_{1+\cdots+1}(21) = 0.4555$). Note that this choice of n_D indicates a risk-averse decision maker. POMICI is built on the theory that the distribution of co-inspections other than j times reveals more information than noise about the incentive to co-inspect the current document j times.

7.2.5 POSICI vs. POMICI—Differences, Similarities, and Improvements

Since both methods are based on a homogeneous group of decision makers modeled by the underlying uniform multivariate distribution, a direct connection between them exists. The sum of the probabilities of all partitions from POMICI with at least one product that was co-inspected exactly j times is equal to the probability in POSICI that

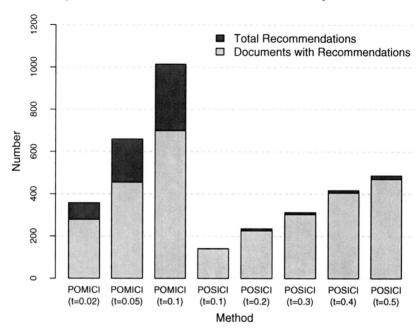

Fig. 7.8. POMICI vs. POSICI. Number of generated recommendations for all documents with $k \leq 15$ on the KVK data for various t

there exists at least one product that was co-inspected exactly j times. In other words, we get from POMICI to POSICI by aggregating all partitions that only differ in the noise area defined in the POSICI underlying preference theory. Thus, Equation 7.15 can also be used instead of the inclusion-exclusion principle to calculate the probability in Equation 7.8.

By setting the threshold t for the POSICI and POMICI algorithms respectively, the number of generated recommendations can be adjusted for both methods. As can be seen in Figure 7.8, when the total number of recommendations is equal, POMICI generally generates longer recommendation lists for fewer documents than POSICI. The POSICI method is stable towards pathological distributions in the input data considering the various factors that influence the amount of generated recommendations (conf. Section 6.6). A larger threshold t will always generate at least as many recommendations as a smaller t-value. This is not the case with POMICI. The two-step-approach of the POMICI algorithm—first choosing partitions and then choosing products out of these partitions—makes POMICI more prone to pathological data. In extreme cases a smaller t-value might produce more recommendations than a larger one. Nothing is said about the quality of the recommendations in this case; a careful consideration of the input data and choice of t should be done. As can be seen on the left hand side of Figure 7.8, in the considered library area, POMICI behaves in a stable and expected way.

POSICI and POMICI are based on different assumptions in the underlying preference theory. To determine which method leads to qualitatively better recommendations in a specific setting the following question has to be answered. When does the partition tail of smaller integers resembles noise and when incentive behavior? One way to answer the question lies in the human evaluation of larger data sets. This is planned for the library application. Groups of different levels of expertise will evaluate datasets of co-inspected documents and determine manually recommendations from these datasets. Then the recommendations of different recommendation generating algorithms will be compared with the manually selected objects.

Two ways to enhance the algorithms appear to be promising. First, if the overall inspection probability of documents is known (through large behavioral data sets), both methods can be extended to be based on an underlying non-uniform multinomial distribution. This can not be applied in the case of a cold start but can be useful in the scenario of very small market baskets covering a large part of the total documents. Second, portraying the additions of further co-purchases ($k \rightarrow k+1$) as a Markov-process enables one to calculate the probability of a product with currently low co-inspections to develop into high co-inspections, thus a reliable recommendation.

7.3 Related Methods

The generation of recommendation methods presented in the previous sections are especially suited to the large samples at STI Providers; recommendation services built around these algorithms will be presented in Chapter 8. By means of examples from these services, Section 8.5.2 will present recommendations of higher order based on the LSD-algorithm and Section 8.5.3 will discuss approaches in the case of non-stationarity. The remainder of this chapter shortly discusses methods, that have been considered for the same kind of data. A general overview on generation of recommendation methods can be found in [AT05]. However, applying traditional recommender approaches is difficult in an STI context. The main two reasons for this are the large number of documents in scientific libraries (10 to 100 million) and the anonymity of users. The number of documents exceeds the number of articles of retailers considerably, even Amazon.com is one order of magnitude smaller.

7.3.1 Collaborative Filtering

One of the first recommender systems was GroupLens [KMM+97] for recommending Usenet news based on user ratings of single news articles and user correlation coefficients. Collaborative filtering methods suffer from the anonymity of user data and inherently high update complexity of correlation coefficients. In addition, the expressiveness of linear product moment correlation coefficients is severely limited. The calculation effort for updating these coefficients is generally $O(n^2)$ in the number of documents in a library which is computationally expensive. A detailed analysis on the evaluation of collaborative filtering recommender systems can be found in [HKTR04].

7.3.2 Regression Models

The main advantage of regression models is that different data sources can be integrated in their model equations; they allow to recommend items based on user attributes as well as product attributes and expert ratings [AEK00, MN02]. However, in a library context the only legal data source is anonymous usage data. This means that in a library context with n objects in the catalog for each document for which recommendations are desired a model must be selected out of 2^{n-1} possible models. In practice the model selection problem is considerably simplified by pruning all variables with a correlation coefficient of zero. However, in the context of a library this still implies the automatic model selection of n models and their estimation. Nevertheless, automatic model selection still is a challenging and difficult task. The currently fastest regression methods still require the inversion of the model's covariance matrix. Both model selection and model estimation require a high computational overhead.

7.3.3 Association Rules

A very popular method to find correlated product groups from market basket data are association rules [AIS93, AS94] and their variants [BMS97, AL99]. A general introduction to association rules can be found in [Ada01]. They have the advantage that no model assumptions need to be made and that they can thus be applied to data of any kind of structure. But they are not very well suited for very large scale data, because of the necessity of making a priori assumptions on thresholds as e. g. support and confidence. In addition both of these parameters depend on total sample size and thus all parameters must be recomputed with every update. For a library context the fact that thresholds are not robust over longer periods of time and must be continuously readjusted to ensure high recommendation quality is a severe disadvantage. The requirement of continuous data analysis for the successful operation of a recommender system is unacceptable for most information providers. The overall performance of the two methods except for grave parameter misspecifications of the association rule method is still very similar. A detailed comparison with the LSD-method from Section 7.1 on the base of usage data from a business-to-business electronics merchant can be found in [GSHT03]; [GSH02] presents a comparison for a business-to-consumer information broker.

7.3.4 Clustering

The use of cluster algorithms for recommender systems has been considered both for preprocessing to reduce the size of large data sets and for the actual generation of recommendations. For a general overview of cluster algorithms, the reader is referred to [Bez81, Boc74, DHS01]. Borchers et al. [BLKR98] state that clustering of items leads to better recommendation quality and improves the scalability of recommender systems. Sarwar et al. [SKKR02], on the other hand, advocate a clustering of the users with the scalable neighborhood algorithm to reach a better scalability. [UF98] proposes to partition both the user and the item set. [FGSN06] presents a method to generate recommendations by means of an algorithm first described in [SSP03]. The method is based on sampling the matrix of co-inspection frequencies using random walks in such a way that during the walks the co-inspection frequencies of subsequent objects increase monotonically. The data accumulated during these walks is then used to identify clusters, based on the idea that document pairs occurring at a later part of a walk are more important than those at an earlier part. In addition, longer walks tend to carry more information than short ones do. The method has been evaluated on data from the University Library of Karlsruhe (see [FGSN06]); due to scalability problems, no recommendation service relying on this method has been opened to the general public so far.

8

Case Study: Behavior-Based Recommender Services for Scientific Libraries

A first behavior-based item-centered recommendation service using browser session input data was introduced in the OPAC of the University Library of Karlsruhe (UBKA) in 2002. In the following years, this system has continuously been improved, evaluated, and additionally set up as external service for different national and international library catalogs. The last major update was the switch to the current web service version (facilitating WSDL, XML and SOAP) in 2006. To answer the question, which co-inspections occur non-random, the algorithms of the previous chapter are applied. Descriptions and evaluations of earlier designs can be found in any of the following contributions: [GSNT03b, GSHNT03c, GSHNT03b, GSHNT03a, GSNT03a]. A more up-to-date service analysis from the customer side including a comparison with the explicit recommendation services presented in Chapter 5 can be found in [Neu07a]. This type of recommender system is best suited to users trying to find standard literature or further readings of a field corresponding to the document they are currently inspecting. Although it does not support the direct interaction (communication) between customers, everybody using the system profits from the actions of other library users.

This chapter describes the current state of the general service, the system architecture and implementation, and different forms of evaluation. Furthermore, it shortly reports on commercializing the service under the BibTip brand as well as on extensions to the existing service.

8.1 Service Description

The service description of the behavior-based recommender system for libraries is divided into two parts. First, the choice and properties of the

Fig. 8.1. Hit list of an OPAC search at the University Library of Karlsruhe

input data are discussed. Second, screen-shots are presented to describe the user interface of this service.

8.1.1 Input Data

In Section 6.3 various possibilities of collecting usage data were discussed. Since bias is the main concern for the data selection, the implicit recommender system portrayed in this chapter is based on browser sessions of users visiting the OPAC. Users generally start by entering search words to look for corresponding documents. This results in getting a list of documents with short titles, author, and year of publication. Figure 8.1 shows the hit list for the search words "economics organization management". The user now has the choice of either going back and altering his search or choosing one document from the hit list by clicking on it. As described in Chapter 6, by choosing one document out of a given set, the user reveals his preference of this document. Clicking on the list opens the detailed document inspection page of the respective item, an example of this kind of page was already shown in Figure 5.1 on page 45. Whenever the user chooses within the same session a document from a hit list—from the same list by going back or

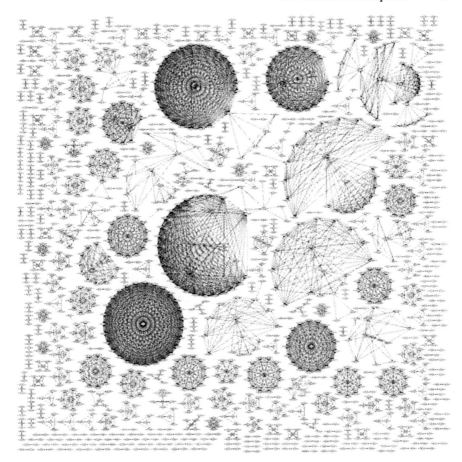

Fig. 8.2. Co-inspection graph of the Karlsruhe Library Portal on 2005-12-20

from a totally different list after a new search—this document is added to the session basket. These co-inspections—documents that have been been inspected by a user within the same session—are the input data of the recommender system.

On a detailed inspection page, the user also has the choice to flip through the hit list by backwards- and forwards-buttons. In these cases, the inspections are not counted for the session basket, because the user revealed no preference: it is not shown, which document will be presented next. Most users prefer not to flip through lists: from 2007-01-01 to 2007-12-21 in the UBKA 1,693,429 times a click on a list was done, the flip mechanism was used only 50,313 times.

By putting all anonymous session baskets together (conf. Chapter 7 for details), an undirected graph of co-inspections is created. The nodes

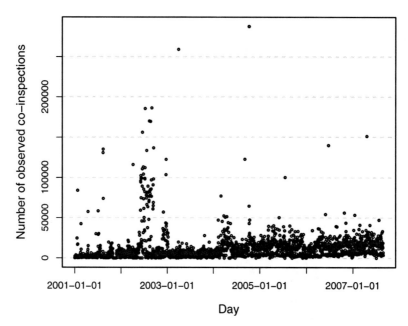

Fig. 8.3. Number of daily observed co-inspections in the UBKA from 2001-01-01 to 2007-09-02

represent inspected items, the edges determine which items have been co-inspected, and the weights describe the number of sessions that contained both documents. Figure 8.2 shows the complete co-inspection graph without weights a few days after the start of the usage observation in the Karlsruhe Library Portal[1], a meta search interface for books and serials in libraries of the region of Karlsruhe. Clearly, many short session of only two or three items can be seen near the border of the graphic, large sessions are presented as complete subgraphs in circular form. In the upper right corner a connected subgraph can be seen that consists of at least five different cliques, most likely stemming from five different sessions.

The input data of the UBKA service comes from two periods. At first, the user sessions were parsed for preprocessing by Perl scripts from Apache log files with link embedded session identifiers. This had one major advantage: before the UBKA recommendation service was started in 2002, older still existing log files starting from 2001-01-01 could be parsed. Thereby, the cold start problem was solved: the new service started with a significant amount of recommendations on the

---
[1] http://www.ubka.uni-karlsruhe.de/kvk/ka_opac/ka_opac_engl.html

first day. Figure 8.3 shows the daily number of observed co-inspections in the UBKA from 2001-01-01 to 2007-09-02. Apache log files were used from 2001 to 2005 as input data. Various changes in the OPAC software led to changes in the session mechanism (e. g. the time out) in this period. Although web robot detection was implemented and the Perl parser was programmed to deal with different session times in public access terminals and to detect session re-starts from bookmarks, the number of co-inspections in Figure 8.3 can still be seen to vary from time to time.

In general, undetected web robots are of no big concern in this application. Web robots do not pass the search input page of the OPAC. The only way for web robots to reach detailed inspection pages is by links to these pages on websites outside the OPAC. Web robots do not browse documents in a meaningful way. Thus, behavioral data of undetected web robots in the OPAC generally qualifies as noise and is successfully filtered out by the algorithms presented in Chapter 7.

After the web service version of the recommender system was introduced in 2006, the input data is homogeneous. Apache log files are not used any more, but the OPAC itself is instructed to prevent robots and write the observed session baskets directly into the database system of the recommendation service. Except for the UBKA, the input data of all other supported STI providers stems completely from the web service version.

8.1.2 User Interface

The behavior-based recommendation service does not have an exclusive starting page in any of the supported STI providers, it is always reached via the detailed document inspection page. The layout of the inspection page depends on the corporate design of the respective library. In most cases, a textual or graphical link to a separate page containing the list of recommendations is presented on the inspection page if and only if recommendations exist. Few library operators prefer to directly present the recommendations on the detailed inspection page. In the UBKA case, the link to the behavior-based recommendations is presented in the topmost line of the user front end of all recommendation services as presented in Figure 5.2 on page 46. Clicking on "Empfehlungen [BibTip]" opens the page with the list of recommendations.

Figure 8.4 shows the recommendation list page of "Three-Dimensional Computer Vision" by Olivier Faugeras (1993). Unfortunately, the UBKA is only available in German. On the left hand side the main document by Faugeras is presented, the list of recommendations is placed

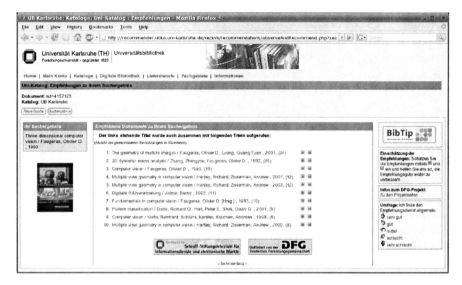

Fig. 8.4. Recommendation list page showing recommendations of "Three-Dimensional Computer Vision" by Olivier Faugeras (1993)

Fig. 8.5. Enlarged cutout of the recommendation list page (Figure 8.4) showing the list of recommendations of "Three-Dimensional Computer Vision" by Olivier Faugeras (1993)

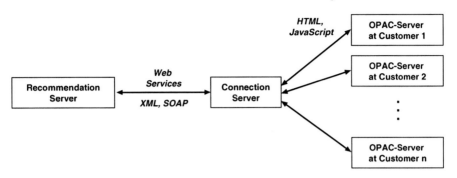

Fig. 8.6. General concept of the architecture of the behavior-based recommendation services

in the center (conf. to Figure 8.5 for an enlarged cutout), and on the right hand side user surveys can be seen that will be discussed in Section 8.3.3. The number of co-inspections of the recommended objects with the main document is given in brackets after each title. The recommender list page can be adapted to the corporate design of the respective library, thus it looks slightly different at all supported STI providers. Clicking on an element of the list of recommendations opens the detailed document inspection page of the respective object.

8.2 Implementation

The implementation of the behavior-based recommender system is portrayed in three parts. First, an overview of the system architecture and software is given. Next, advantages that result from the distributed design are discussed. And last, the control interfaces for the management of the system by the operator are presented.

8.2.1 System Architecture

Figure 8.6 shows the general concept of the architecture of the behavior-based recommendation service. The recommender system resides on two logical servers. The connection server speaks to the customers: it collects the behavioral data and creates the web pages with the recommendation lists. The recommendation server speaks to the connection server only: it requests the observed co-inspections, computes the recommendations, and sends these back to the connection server.

All internal components of the recommender system employ the Simple Object Access Protocol (SOAP) [BEK+00] to communicate

Table 8.1. SOAP message with recommendation list in XML format (abridged)

```
<?xml version="1.0" encoding="utf-8"?>
<soap:Envelope xmlns:xsi="http://www.w3.org/2001/XMLSchema-instance"
        xmlns:soapenc="http://schemas.xmlsoap.org/soap/encoding/"
        xmlns:xsd="http://www.w3.org/2001/XMLSchema"
        soap:encodingStyle="http://schemas.xmlsoap.org/soap/encoding/"
        xmlns:soap="http://schemas.xmlsoap.org/soap/envelope/">
  <soap:Body>
    <getRecommendationsResponse xmlns="urn:KVKRec">
      <requestedDocument xmlns:types="urn:KVKRec:DataTypes"
                         xsi:type="types:documentIdentifier">
        <ID xsi:type="xsd:string">4157123</ID>
        <catalog xsi:type="xsd:string">UBKA</catalog>
      </requestedDocument>
      <recommendations xmlns:types="urn:KVKRec:DataTypes"
                       xsi:type="types:arrayOfRecommendations">
        <item xmlns:types="urn:KVKRec:DataTypes"
             xsi:type="types:recommendation">
          <document xmlns:types="urn:KVKRec:DataTypes"
                    xsi:type="types:documentIdentifier">
            <ID xsi:type="xsd:string">10172544</ID>
            <catalog xsi:type="xsd:string">UBKA</catalog>
          </document>
          <buys xsi:type="xsd:integer">8</buys>
        </item>
        ...
        <item xmlns:types="urn:KVKRec:DataTypes"
             xsi:type="types:recommendation">
          <document xmlns:types="urn:KVKRec:DataTypes"
                    xsi:type="types:documentIdentifier">
            <ID xsi:type="xsd:string">9061290</ID>
            <catalog xsi:type="xsd:string">UBKA</catalog>
          </document>
          <buys xsi:type="xsd:integer">34</buys>
        </item>
      </recommendations>
    </getRecommendationsResponse>
  </soap:Body>
</soap:Envelope>
```

with each other. SOAP was chosen for its independence from programming language, platform and transport mechanism. This and the multitude of freely available SOAP implementations allow to facilitate different programming languages for different tasks and problems. Having this freedom of choice concerning the programming language makes it possible to offer recommender services to partners without enforcing a certain technical infrastructure. The actual data is sent in XML format via SOAP. As an example, Table 8.1 shows the SOAP message including the recommendation list in XML format which corresponds to the recommendation list page depicted in Figure 8.4 on page 96.

Furthermore, the Web Services Description Language (WSDL) [CCMW01] is used to define data types and interfaces. WSDL descriptions provide a solid specification, which allows to replace single components without making global modifications. This has proven very useful in the realm of data collection, where it was possible to easily add different sources. As an example, Table 8.2 shows the WSDL file residing on the recommendation server which defines the format of the recommendation list message depicted in Table 8.1.

The behavioral data is collected by JavaScript code embedded in the OPAC detailed inspection page. The script reports every view of a document with timestamp and session identifier to an observation daemon written in PHP. In the next step preprocessing is applied, the data is grouped by sessions, and sets of co-inspections are generated and made accessible via a SOAP service also implemented in PHP.

The provided baskets are then retrieved by the recommendation server via SOAP and written to an intermediate database table. After the retrieval, the recommender system is triggered to update its recommendations. The generated recommendations can again be queried using a SOAP interface. The recommendation server is implemented in Perl using SOAP::Lite for communication, the connection server is programmed in PHP 5 with the PHP Data Objects (PDO) extension. Both are running on Linux, use PostgreSQL as the database system and the Apache HTTP Server as the web server. Thus, the complete recommender system is built on open source software.

Currently all supported catalogs are updated daily in the night at times of low user traffic. The current implementation features incremental updates with a complexity of $O(n^2)$ in time and space with n the number of items co-inspected in the update period. Only for inspected documents the recommendations are re-computed. Since the upper bound is reduced by a reduction of the update period, this improves the scalability of the algorithm.

Table 8.2. WSDL defining the recommendation list SOAP message (abridged)

```xml
<?xml version="1.0" encoding="UTF-8"?>
<wsdl:definitions
  name="KVKRec"
  targetNamespace="urn:KVKRec"
  xmlns:soap="http://schemas.xmlsoap.org/wsdl/soap/"
  xmlns:tns="urn:KVKRec"
  xmlns:types="urn:KVKRec:DataTypes"
  xmlns:wsdl="http://schemas.xmlsoap.org/wsdl/"
  xmlns:xsd="http://www.w3.org/2001/XMLSchema">
  <wsdl:types>
    <xsd:schema
      targetNamespace="urn:KVKRec:DataTypes"
      xmlns:SOAP-ENC="http://schemas.xmlsoap.org/soap/encoding/"
      xmlns:types="urn:KVKRec:DataTypes"
      ...
    <xsd:complexType name="documentIdentifier">
      <xsd:annotation>
        <xsd:documentation>Unique identifier comprising a catalog and
                          an id</xsd:documentation>
      </xsd:annotation>
      <xsd:sequence>
        <xsd:element maxOccurs="1" minOccurs="1" name="catalog"
                    type="xsd:string"/>
        <xsd:element maxOccurs="1" minOccurs="1" name="ID"
                    type="xsd:string"/>
      </xsd:sequence>
    </xsd:complexType>
    <xsd:complexType name="recommendation">
      <xsd:annotation>
        <xsd:documentation>A recommendation consisting of a document
                          and the number of buys</xsd:documentation>
      </xsd:annotation>
      <xsd:sequence>
        <xsd:element maxOccurs="1" minOccurs="1" name="document"
                    type="types:documentIdentifier"/>
        <xsd:element maxOccurs="1" minOccurs="1" name="buys"
                    type="xsd:integer"/>
      </xsd:sequence>
    </xsd:complexType>
    <xsd:complexType name="arrayOfRecommendations">
      <xsd:annotation>
        <xsd:documentation>A list of
                          recommendations</xsd:documentation>
      </xsd:annotation>
```

Table 8.2. (continued)

```
      <xsd:complexContent>
        <xsd:restriction base="SOAP-ENC:Array">
          <xsd:sequence>
            <xsd:element maxOccurs="unbounded" minOccurs="0"
                         name="item" type="types:recommendation"/>
          </xsd:sequence>
          <xsd:attribute ref="SOAP-ENC:arrayType"
                         wsdl:arrayType="types:recommendation[]"/>
        </xsd:restriction>
      </xsd:complexContent>
    </xsd:complexType>
  </xsd:schema>
</wsdl:types>
<wsdl:message name="getRecommendationsResponse">
  <wsdl:part name="requestedDocument"
             type="types:documentIdentifier"/>
  <wsdl:part name="recommendations"
             type="types:arrayOfRecommendations"/>
</wsdl:message>
...
<wsdl:portType name="KVKRecPortType">
  <wsdl:operation name="getRecommendations">
    <wsdl:input message="tns:getRecommendations"/>
    <wsdl:output message="tns:getRecommendationsResponse"/>
  </wsdl:operation>
  ...
</wsdl:portType>
<wsdl:binding name="KVKRecBinding" type="tns:KVKRecPortType">
  <soap:binding style="rpc"
                transport="http://schemas.xmlsoap.org/soap/http"/>
  <wsdl:operation name="getRecommendations">
    <soap:operation soapAction="urn:KVKRec#getRecommendations"/>
    <wsdl:input>
      <soap:body namespace="urn:KVKRec" parts="document"
                 use="literal"/>
    </wsdl:input>
    <wsdl:output>
      <soap:body namespace="urn:KVKRec"
                 parts="requestedDocument recommendations"
                 use="literal"/>
    </wsdl:output>
  </wsdl:operation>
  ...
</wsdl:binding>
<wsdl:service name="KVKRec">
  <wsdl:port binding="tns:KVKRecBinding" name="KVKRecPort">
```

Table 8.2. (continued)

```
<soap:address location=
  "http://ubrec.em.uni-karlsruhe.de/cgi-bin/UBRecSoapServer"/>
 </wsdl:port>
 </wsdl:service>
</wsdl:definitions>
```

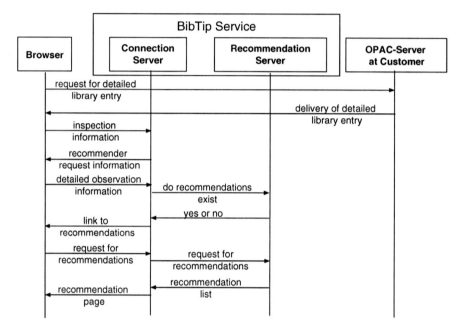

Fig. 8.7. Message trace for detailed view and recommendation request

Figure 8.7 shows the message trace triggered by the browser of a user who requests a detailed view of a document (see Figure 5.1 on page 45) and then visits the recommendation list page for this item (see Figure 8.4 on page 96). On the recommendation server, the design of the database features special purpose tables for the seen requests. For example, a special table exists for fast look-ups about the existence of recommendations for a requested document.

The data of each customer is handled separately in the database. The recommendations for one customer are generated out of the usage data of the very same customer only. The integration of the service on the customer side is done by adding three segments to the HTML-code of the detailed inspection page of the OPAC of the customer:

• Div tags to store values for ISXN, short-title, and internal id

Table 8.3. Example of the HTML-source-code of a detailed document view including behavior-based recommendations (abridged)

```
<body>

  ...web page content of detailed view...

<div id="bibtip_isxn" style="display:none">0-13-224650-3</div>
<div id="bibtip_shorttitle" style="display:none">Economics,
              organization and management / Milgrom, Paul , 1992</div>
<div id="bibtip_id" style="display:none">2654629</div>

  ...web page content of detailed view...

<script
  src="http://recommender.ubka.uni-karlsruhe.de/js/bibtip_ubka.js"
  type="text/javascript"></script>

  ...web page content of detailed view...

<div style="display:none" id="bibtip_reclist"></div>

  ...web page content of detailed view...

</body>
```

- A script tag with the BibTip JavaScript URL as source attribute
- A div tag to determine the place for inserting the recommendation list or the link to the recommendation list

Table 8.3 shows as an example the integration of the recommender service into the detailed document inspection page of Milgrom and Roberts [MR92] in the OPAC of the UBKA.

8.2.2 Advantages of the Distributed Design

The advantages of the described design lie in its scalability and its universality. The scalability stems from the clean separation of concerns which allows to divide work among multiple computers. By using web services built upon SOAP, content aware multilayer switches can be used to balance the load among similarly configured servers. Furthermore, the time-consuming task of calculating recommendations has no effect on the performance or availability of the web service that delivers recommendations to the client. The main reason for this is that the estimation of the stochastic processes and the outlier detection can be decoupled from the delivery process of recommendations. Delivering recommendations stays as simple as an indexed look-up on a database table, keeping the process fast and easy. Without taking the time for network connection initiation into account, it takes less than 50 ms to deliver the recommendations for a document, even though the system within the OPAC of the University Library of Karlsruhe contains nearly 3 million individual recommendations, which are calculated from more than 33 million observations.

While scalability ensures that the system can be used by an arbitrary number of users in parallel, universality of the system not only allows to add new interfaces—the next chapter of this work presents the alternative RecoDiver interface—but, on a different level, completely independent catalogs as well. Although this chapter focuses on the installation for the OPAC at Karlsruhe, this is only one example of different parallel services that are provided through the same infrastructure. Currently, 23 information providers (including international meta and compound library catalogs) with separated data sources, calculation of recommendations, and custom interfaces featuring their own corporate design are supported. The commercial service BibTip presented in Section 8.4 will further increase the number of independent supported catalogs.

8.2.3 System Operator Control Interface

The systems architecture enables the start of recommendation services for new clients (information providers) with minimal effort. Adding an independent service for a new information provider as described in the previous section is done by inserting its service name in one single configuration file on the recommendation server. This results in automatic creation of independent database space and web services, thereby, recommendations for this client are generated and presented only on the basis of its own usage data.

For controlling the recommender system different tools were developed to guaranty a high service rate by enhancing the overall reliability. All services are automatically polled every minute from servers outside of the general recommender system architecture to check for service interruptions or delays. Any response problems are pushed by email to the system operator. These requests are not counted for usage analysis. In addition to the available standard features of servers two web front ends for the system operator were developed.

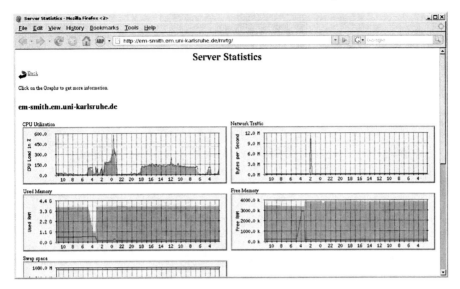

Fig. 8.8. Recommendation server monitoring of network traffic and machine parameters

First, network traffic and several machine parameters are monitored constantly and are graphically processed for inspection with the mrtg package[2]. It allows the visual inspection on daily, weekly, and monthly basis of the following parameters: CPU utilization, network traffic, used memory and swap, as well as disk space on the connected RAIDs (Redundant Arrays of Independent Disks). Figure 8.8 shows a small part of this interface as an example. The nightly recommendations update and database security back-up are easily identified.

Second, a much more complex interface was implemented in Perl for the surveillance of the update process, the generated recommendations, and the usage. Under the categories of "process quality", "service usage", "user acceptance", and "professional evaluation" it allows for separate catalogs a fast inspection of the most relevant service parameters: gathered usage data, number of recommendations and lists, recommendation service requests on different time bases, SOAP request parameters, most requested recommendations, products with the most recommendations, time and data space of the last recommendation updates, as well as graphical visualization of the votes of ongoing user evaluations. As an example, Figure 8.9 shows a small part of this interface depicting the nightly updates of the UBKA catalog.

---

[2] http://www.mrtg.org

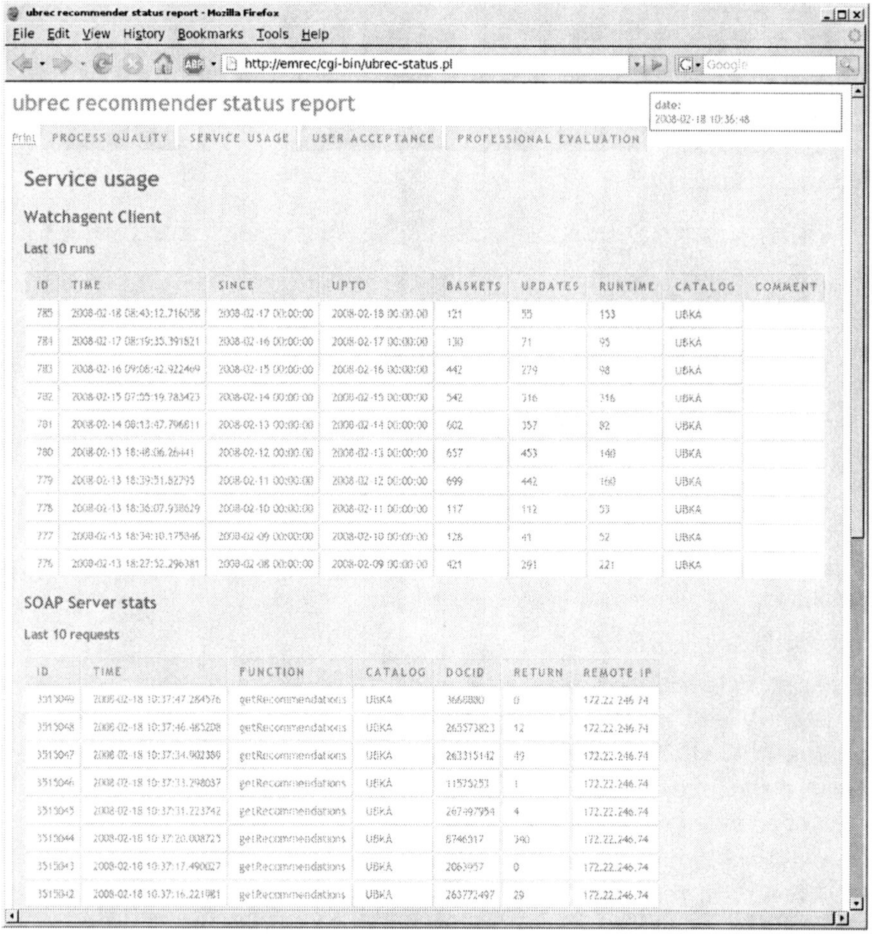

Fig. 8.9. System operator monitoring tool for recommendation statistics

8.3 Evaluation

Although the described implicit recommender system is integrated as external services in currently eleven library catalogs, this evaluation focuses mainly on the UBKA service. The UBKA was the first supported catalog and allowed the integration of user surveys, which is not possible in most of the others catalogs due to restrictions by the respective library managers.

The evaluation is divided into four parts. First, statistical properties of the generated recommendations are given. Second, the usage of the service is discussed. Third, the results of the user surveys are presented. And fourth, the diffusion of recommendations in the UBKA is analyzed.

Table 8.4. Statistics of the computation of recommendation lists in the UBKA for the observation period 2001-01-01 to 2007-12-26

	I q undef.	II no χ^2 (< 3 classes)	III Sign. $\alpha = 0.05$	IV Sign. $\alpha = 0.01$	V Not sign.	$\sum$
A Obs. < 10	128,768 (0)	19,070 (3,404)	0 (0)	0 (0)	0 (0)	147,838 (3,404)
B $\bar{x} = 1$	137,349 (0)	0 (0)	0 (0)	0 (0)	0 (0)	137,349 (0)
C $\bar{x} > \sigma^2$ $r \leq 3$	1,161 (0)	126,152 (30,950)	654 (529)	1,419 (1,140)	12,993 (6,586)	142,379 (39,205)
D $\bar{x} > \sigma^2$ $r > 3$	0 (0)	31,712 (31,674)	5,469 (5,469)	2,472 (2,472)	48,777 (47,575)	88,430 (87,190)
E $\sigma^2 > \bar{x}$	0 (0)	20,998 (20,998)	20,080 (20,080)	6,284 (6,284)	47,979 (47,979)	95,341 (95,341)
$\sum$	267,278 (0)	197,932 (87,026)	26,203 (26,078)	10,175 (9,896)	109,749 (102,140)	611,337 (225,140)

(n) denotes n lists of recommendations

8.3.1 Recommendation Statistics

Table 8.4 summarizes the statistical results of the computation of recommendation lists in the UBKA by means of the LSD-algorithm for the observation period 2001-01-01 to 2007-12-26. On the left hand side a classification according to the co-inspections can be seen, on the top a classification according to the χ^2-goodness-of-fit test is given (conf. Table 7.2 on page 77). 611,337 of the overall quantity of 929,637 documents have been inspected by users in a session together with at least one other document. A total of 33,452,367 user inspections were observed. From these data 225,140 lists with recommendations have been generated with a total number of 2,915,168 recommendations. Thus, the average length of a recommendation list is 12.9 documents.

As Table 8.4 shows, recommendations are identified with this model even if the LSD-model estimated can not be tested for significance (column II of Table 8.4) or if the LSD-model is not significant (column V of Table 8.4). The reason for this is that the LSD-model is used as an approximation of an underlying stationary stochastic purchase process

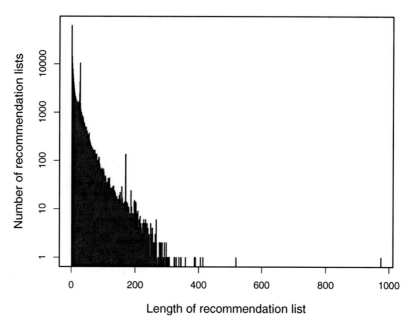

Fig. 8.10. Distribution of the length of recommendation lists on a logarithmic scale in the UBKA on 2007-12-26

which is removed in order to present the non-random outliers as recommendations. Especially for documents observed over a longer period of time, combinations with documents recently bought by the library obviously violate assumptions underlying the LSD-model, because pairs with a recently bought document had a smaller chance to be inspected together in a session than pairs of older documents. Nevertheless, for relatively short time periods and periods of small library growth, the LSD-model holds to be a robust first approximation and thus a useful filter of randomness.

Figure 8.10 shows the distribution of the length of recommendation lists on a logarithmic scale in the UBKA on 2007-12-26. Two outliers can be seen. The longest recommendation list consists of 975 objects. This list belongs to the general "Lecture notes in computer science" series of Springer (Berlin, Heidelberg, New York), which is published since 1973 and available in electronic form through a site license of the University Library of Karlsruhe. The second longest list with 520 items belongs to a German introductory mathematics course book that seems to be used by most students in the technical fields of the Universität Karlsruhe (TH). While lists of this length will not be browsed completely by users, the average list length of 12.9 items can easily be inspected.

Since the usage distribution of documents in nearly every library is highly skewed (newer documents, or documents to topics that interest a large part of the overall library users, in general are more requested), many recommendations will be generated for documents that are used often while seldom used documents have fewer or no recommendations. Of the 929,637 documents in the catalog, 225,140 documents have lists with recommendations, a total of 2,915,168 recommendations exist. Because of the skewness, the coverage of actual detailed document inspections is 74.9% (much higher than the coverage of the complete catalog). So the probability that recommendations exist for a document a user is currently interested in is 0.749.

8.3.2 Usage

The usage of the service, at least all SOAP requests to the recommendation server, are logged in database tables for statistical analysis. From 2007-01-01 to 2007-12-21 the users of the UBKA inspected 1,693,429 detailed document inspection pages. This is equal to the number of SOAP requests the connection server sent to the recommendation server asking for the existence of recommendations. In 425,803 cases, no recommendations for the inspected documents were available; in 1,267,626 cases a list of recommendations existed, thus the link to the recommendation page was shown on the detailed document page. This is the previously mentioned service availability rate of 0.749. 11,473 times the users clicked on the link to open the recommendations list page. In 57 percent of the cases a user requested the list of recommendations, a click on one of the recommendations is reported.

Regarding these numbers, the difference of the only one percent click-rate to open the list but the 57 percent usage rate of the recommendations in the list is striking. While a click-rate of one percent is comparable to many such systems in e-commerce, it is not necessarily satisfying for the system operator. Two possible explanation models exists. Under the assumption, that the behavior-based recommender service is widely known among the potential users, these number can be interpreted as follows: the majority of the users does not consider the service to be useful, thus ignoring it; a minority considers the service as useful, thus requests from time to time the list of recommendations and then in most cases, clicks on one of the recommendations. Two problems with this model arise. First, the next section will show that the users in general are quite content with the service. Second, surveys

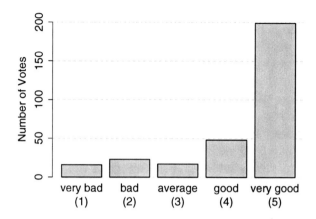

Fig. 8.11. Histogram of the distribution of user votes about the general quality of the UBKA recommendation service from 2005-03-23 to 2007-12-21

in lectures have shown that the service is actually nearly completely unknown among students. Thus, the low click-rate of one percent seems to stem from the lack of knowledge about the existence of the service.

The question remains, why the service is unknown. Here, the argumentation from Section 5.5.2 can be repeated. The link to the behavior-based recommendation service is "hidden" in a list of other links on the side on the page. Only recently, the BibTip icon has been added and the link has been moved to the first place in the second box on the right hand side of the detailed inspection page (conf. Figure 5.1 on page 45). Before this change, the link to the service was the word "Empfehlungen", which appeared in the ninth line of similarly looking bibliographic links like "titles from the same author". A user had to scan all lines at each inspection page to see, if the link is there showing that recommendations exist. In other libraries and library meta catalogs that have signed up for the BibTip service, the link will be shown in a more prominent place. This might allow in the future to better judge the importance of lucid user interfaces for this service.

8.3.3 User Surveys

For collecting the single subjective impressions and opinions of the users of the system two surveys have been placed next to the recommendation list. One allows to give opinions about the service in general, the other about single recommendations.

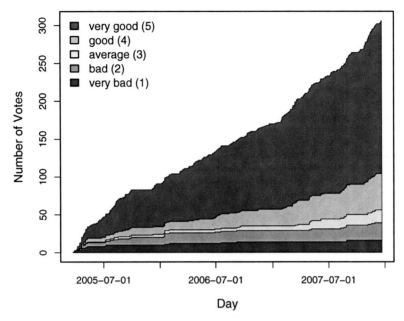

Fig. 8.12. Area chart of the history of user votes about the general quality of the UBKA recommendation service from 2005-03-23 to 2007-12-21

Since March 2005 in the UBKA an online survey asking "I consider the recommendation service in general: (Ich finde den Empfehlungs-dienst allgemein:)" is placed alongside the list of recommendations as can be seen on the right hand side of Figure 8.4 on page 96. On a five item Likert scale the possible answers are (1) very bad, (2) bad, (3) average, (4) good, and (5) very good. The results of this survey, which are depicted in Figure 8.11, show that users are generally very content with the existing service. 303 user votes with a mean of 4.29 and a variance of 1.41 have been collected. The distribution of the votes and thereby the mean as well has been very stable over the time of the observation period. Figure 8.12 shows the growth history of the votes from 2005-03-23 to 2007-12-21.

The users are able to submit their opinions about single recommendations as well. This can be done by means of the "+" and "−" icons next to each list entry as seen in Figure 8.4 on page 96. The explanation of this feature on the right hand side of the website mentions that the user can thereby help to improve the quality of recommendations. Figure 8.13 shows the results of this survey. This data is currently collected for survey purposes only. Due to its design, it is not an objective

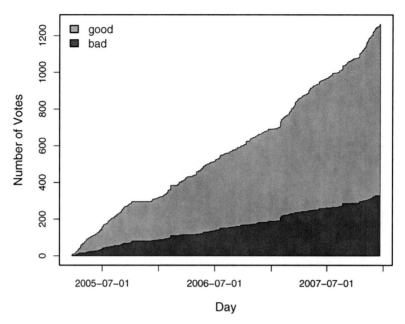

Fig. 8.13. Area chart of the history of user votes about single recommendations of the UBKA recommendation service from 2005-03-23 to 2007-12-21

survey about the quality of recommendations. Most likely, users will often only use the service to mark recommendations that are not correct in their opinion. At the time of writing, this data is not used in any way for the generation of the recommendations, the system is strictly behavior-based. It remains to be determined, if mixing this explicit information with the collected implicit behavioral data will improve the overall recommendation quality.

8.3.4 Diffusion of Recommendations

The amount of observed co-inspections in the UBKA that is used as the input to the recommendation generating algorithms has been discussed in Section 8.1.1 and shown in Figure 8.3 on page 94. Changes in the mechanism to determine the browser session of a single user and restructurings in the library catalog design have lead to measurable changes of the statistical properties of the input data. This has influences on the diffusion of recommendations as has been discussed in Section 6.6. Figure 8.14 shows the number of products with recommendation lists in the UBKA from 2001-01-01 to 2007-09-02; Figure 8.15 depicts the growth of the total number of recommendations in the

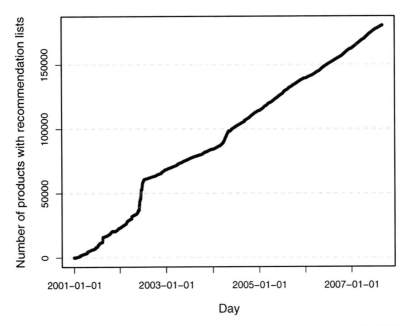

Fig. 8.14. Number of products with recommendation lists in the UBKA from 2001-01-01 to 2007-09-02

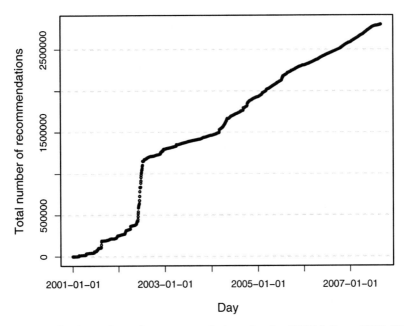

Fig. 8.15. Total number of recommendations in the UBKA from 2001-01-01 to 2007-09-02

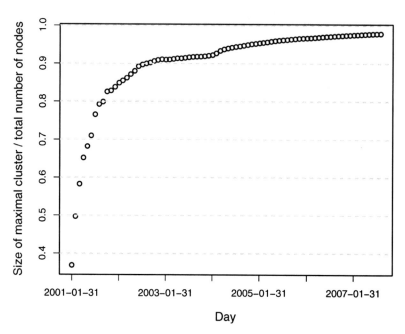

Fig. 8.16. Size of the maximal cluster / total number of nodes in the UBKA co-inspection graph at the end of each month from Jan. 2001 to Sep. 2007

UBKA in the same period. In the years 2001 to 2005 various changes of the diffusion speed can be seen. The introduction of the web service version of the recommender system in 2006 improved the reliability and consistency of the input data. In 2006 and 2007 the number of recommendations has grown in a steady rate.

Besides the number of recommendations, the distribution of recommendations among the products is relevant. This can be measured be analyzing the graph of recommendations. The general setup of such a graph has been discussed in Section 8.1.1 by means of the example of Figure 8.2 on page 93. On 2007-09-30, the co-inspection graph of the UBKA consisted of 509,201 items, the recommendation graph had 178,568 nodes. Figure 8.16 shows the growth of the quotient of the size of the maximal cluster divided by the total number of nodes in the co-inspection graph of the UBKA at the end of each month from January 2001 to September 2007. Figure 8.17 shows the same quotient for the recommendation graph. With more and more behavioral data on the nearly stationary set of documents of the library, the discussed quotient of the co-inspections graph tends to 1—on 2007-09-30 it was 0.979 (the maximal cluster consisted of 498,478 nodes). The growth rate

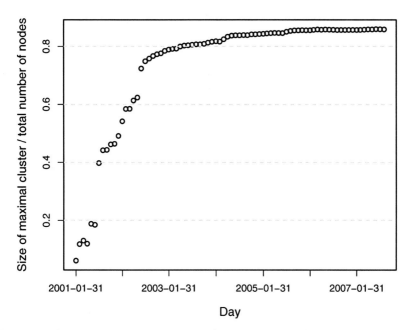

Fig. 8.17. Size of the maximal cluster / total number of nodes in the UBKA recommendation graph at the end of each month from Jan. 2001 to Sep. 2007

of the quotient in the recommendation graph has significantly slowed down at 0.858 on 2007-09-30 (the maximal cluster consisted of 153,269 nodes). Thus, displaying the recommendations as a graph means foremost to somehow visualize the largest cluster. Chapter 9 will go into more detail on this problem.

8.4 BibTip: Commercial Implicit Recommendation Services for Libraries

The behavior-based recommendation service at the University Library of Karlsruhe and Karlsruhe's Virtual Catalog got large attention within the library community. Thus, it was decided to bring the service to the market. The service is offered to libraries worldwide under the BibTip brand[3] with the University Library of Karlsruhe as the main contact. A growing international customer base has already been installed. The connection server resides at the library; the library staff manages the customer support. The recommendation server at the chair of information services and electronic markets computes the recommendations

---

[3] http://www.bibtip.org

and speaks only to the connection server via the previously described web services. The customers pay a yearly fee for the provision of the service. The integration of the service on the customers side is done by only adding three segments to the HTML-code of the OPAC to connect in an AJAX like technique as described in Section 8.2.1.

8.5 Extensions, Improvements, and Further Applications

Several extensions, improvements, and further applications of the portrayed recommender system are possible.

The list-based user interface seen in Figure 8.4 is easy to understand but very limited for grasping the whole graph of recommendations. Chapter 9 discusses an alternative graph-based user interface for the behavior-based recommendation service.

While many software applications for product management in traditional retail or e-commerce stores exist, collection management at libraries still mostly relies on the knowledge of the librarians and requests from patrons. Usage data from an implicit recommender system connected with the metadata of the documents are a very good basis for more advanced approaches. Repeat-buying models aggregated at the level of document categories could be used for implementing a more customer centric collection policy.

In the remainder of this section, first an e-mail notification service to extend the communication channels to the users of the recommender system is discussed. Second, recommendations of higher order relying on more than one item-to-item relationship are depicted. And finally, an outlook for taking product life cycles into account for the generation of recommendations is given.

8.5.1 Push E-Mail Notification Service

A push e-mail notification service was added to the recommender system. It was accessible through a link on the top of the recommendation list page. Users with a library account received an e-mail including a direct link to the recommendation page if new recommendations appeared for a previously specified document. The usage of this service did not meet the first expectations. Users seem to be skeptic about any service that tries to grab their attention—like spam mails—at times when they do not even visit the library. Due to privacy concerns about the user accounts, the service was hosted by the University Library of Karlsruhe and accessed the recommendation server via a web service considering the generation date of every single recommendation in the history. The service was canceled in 2007. It is planned to relaunch this notification service in the near future by means of RSS feed techniques. Thereby, each user can decide within the RSS reader when to poll the service. Further on, this way it is no longer connected to existing user accounts, but opened as a personalized service to the general public.

8.5.2 Higher Order Recommendations

So far, information products related to one single item have been considered. Recommendations of higher order are items that are related to a set of other items. For example, by analyzing the click-stream within one user session a set of products relevant to the user can be determined; the items placed in a virtual shopping cart at an e-commerce site is a relevant set as well for presenting additional products during the check-out process. The more items that are relevant for a specific user are known—this can be considered as the profile of an anonymous user—the more specific and useful recommendations can be given. The algorithms presented in Chapter 7 generalize to higher order associations in a straight-forward way.

With millions of products, computing recommendations for all possible sets is very space and time consuming. Even the number of all existing two-item-sets in the usage data can be very large in highly connected co-inspection graphs. To limit the number of statistical models that have to be computed, higher order recommendations can also be presented out of the data of single item recommendations. Figure 8.18 shows the complete recommendation graph of Karlsruhe's Virtual Catalog (conf. Section 7.2.1) a few days after the start of the recommendation service for this meta library catalog. In the nodes, the ISXNs of the products are given; the weights of the edges are the number of co-inspections; a directed edge points to an item recommended as additional reading to the father node. Clearly, some fully connected subgraphs of three and four items can be seen. When a user has inspected any subset of nodes of a fully connected subgraph, all other nodes within this subgraph can be presented as recommendations.

8.5.3 Non-Stationary Regime

The LSD-Algorithm presented in Section 7.1 is based on the assumption of stationarity, although even Ehrenberg stressed that this only has to hold for currently examined products within a possible short analysis

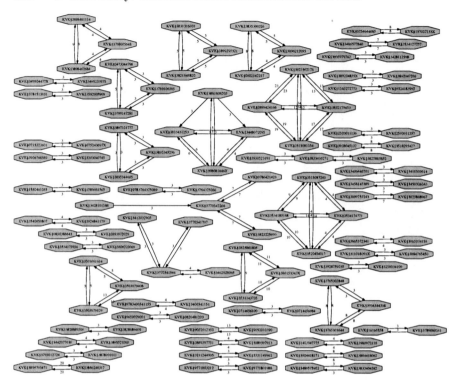

Fig. 8.18. Recommendation graph of Karlsruhe's Virtual Catalog on 2006-06-07

period. When information products are available for longer time periods, a non-stationary regime for these products can be assumed. This gives way for taking product life cycles into account for the generation of recommendations. The general life time of products even depends on the scientific discipline. For example, computer science books dealing with a specific version of a programming language or software in general have a shorter life time than history documentaries or introductions to abstract algebra. On the basis of usage data, product growth models (e. g. Bass' model [Bas69] with its many successors) can be computed and the growth model can be used for weighting the inspections. Product B, which has been co-inspected with product A 30 times in the last three months might be a better recommendation to A than Product C, which has been co-inspected with product A 500 times in the last 10 years but is in its last life stage.

This implies that one could first identify documents with a short life cycle like e. g. those on the previous fashionable programming technology and, based on this classification, attenuate or even remove rec-

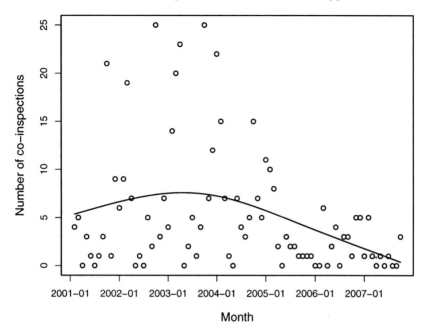

Fig. 8.19. Monthly co-inspections of the document pair (6262739,5368367) from February 2001 to October 2007 in the UBKA catalog with a fitted cubic spline

ommendations to these books on the now obsolete technology from the recommendation list. Alternatively, the life cycle phase of a document could be presented in the user interface. Iconic labels could e. g. convey information like "A classic on this subject" or "Obsolete" to the user.

As a generalization, life cycles of sets of products can be considered. Figure 8.19 shows the monthly co-inspections of a pair of computer science books from February 2001 to October 2007 in the UBKA with a fitted cubic spline. The spline hints that the relationship of these two books is coming to the end of its life cycle. Currently, different recommendation generating algorithms regarding life cycles are developed and evaluated to be applied for the behavior-based recommendation service presented in this chapter.

Analyzing the usage of document sets defined by content classifications through library metadata (title words, keywords, library classifications, etc.) even makes it possible to identify general reading trends and thereby trends in their respective scientific area. Life cycle analysis might become an important tool for the previously mentioned collection management at libraries.

9

Visualizing and Exploring Information Spaces

The previous chapters showed that behavior-based systems play a major role within the variety of recommender systems. The general interface approach of these systems is to present a list of products that are either related to the customer's purchase (or inspection) history or have been co-purchased by other customers together with the product of current interest. This interface has two main advantages: it is easily understood and easily integrated by HTML lists or tables into the shop website. The large drawback of this presentation is that the customer is completely unaware of the overall connections between the products. Conceptually, behavior-based recommendations are the weighted edges of a digraph with the products as nodes. In its most common form, the weight of an edge presents the amount of co-purchases of the two products associated with the nodes connected by the edge. Users could significantly benefit from a more advanced user interface presenting this kind of connection. This becomes even more clear in the case of new products with few recommendations due to the small amount of behavioral data gathered so far. A new product might only have three (first level) recommendations, while the recommended three products might each have ten different recommendations, i.e. a total of 30 second level recommendations of the new product assuming disjunctive sets of recommendations. A direct presentation of the subgraph of the first and second level recommendations (a total of 33 products in this example) is more useful than just presenting direct neighbors of the graph (first level recommendations) and leaving the back and forth browsing to detect the second order neighbors to the customers.

This chapter presents and evaluates a tool to dynamically browse such a network of recommendations. First, an overview of existing visual interfaces to information providers is given. Then, RecoDiver, a new graph-based user interface to recommendations is presented, evaluated, and discussed. More Information on RecoDiver can be found in [NPR08].

9.1 A Survey of Visual Interfaces to Information Providers

Since the 1990s an extensive amount of research has been conducted on visual interfaces to information providers, especially digital libraries [Shi07]. The search and retrieval activities supported by such interfaces include the formulation and modification of search queries, the cognition of the structure and content of search results, browsing to gain an overview of the coverage of a digital collection, and understanding how the retrieved documents are related to one another [BC02]. This section discusses a number of existing visual interfaces. While some have focused on a single one of these activities, most have tried to deal with more than one activity at once.

Fowler et al. [FFW91] present a document retrieval system that integrates query, thesaurus, and documents through a common visual representation, namely fisheye views and overview diagrams of thesaurus terms and bibliographic elements. The user may formulate and modify queries and visualize search results using a unified interface. Jones [Jon98] presents VQuery, a query interface which exploits Venn-like diagrams for query formulation as an alternative to the commonly used Boolean logic in textual queries. Envision [FHN+93, NFH+96] provides its search results as scatterplots of various bibliographic attributes, e. g. authors and publication date. Users may directly manipulate a number of parameters of such scatterplots in order to find the relevant literature. The interface presented in [MHML05] also employs scatterplots to represent sets of objects in digital libraries using metadata fields and citation data. VisMeB [KRML03] is a metadata visualization system that aims at improving the process of finding relevant information in an intuitive yet multifunctional way. It uses scatterplots, pie and bar charts, along with so-called SuperTables. The idea of using multiple coordinated views is also reflected in MedioVis [GGJ+05], a visual information seeking system that consists of scatterplots, tables, and spatial representations. Its main goal is to simplify the user's process of information retrieval and thus encouraging the use of the library. In addition to scatterplots, the Informedia project [Chr02] has developed two visualization techniques to access a multi-terabyte digital video library, namely timelines and maps, which allow the user direct manipulation of the information displayed. The graphical user interfaces developed for the BalticSeaWeb project [LN98] also allow to restrict the search to a certain region by selecting a particular area on a map. A different direction is pursued by [HKW94, BST98, FR98]. These systems enable the user to navigate through the information space of documents which are interconnected by relevance, i.e. similar keywords. Sebrechts et al. [SCL+99] present NIRVE, a tool that supports 3D and 2D visualizations of search results along with a textual representation. The three different interfaces were evaluated against each other. Their experimental results showed that only under the right combination of task, user, and interface did the 3D visualization result in a similar performance than comparable 2D and textual tools. LibViewer [RB99] uses metaphor graphics to display information about the documents in a digital library in an intuitive way, i.e. sets of documents are arranged on a virtual bookshelf using different colors, sizes, formats, etc. Similarly, the NSDL Virtual Spine Viewer [Dus04] allows to explore both certain subjects and search results by browsing scatterplots of virtual book spines. Sumner et al. [SBAG03, BBS06] proposed a conceptual browsing interface for educational digital libraries based on semantic-spatial maps called strand maps. Such strand maps provide a visual organization of relevant conceptual information in order to promote the use of science content during digital library use. The fluid interface proposed in [GPJB05] visualizes document collections in a digital library via zoomable treemaps. In addition, the integrated document reader allows for intuitive navigation between multiple documents in a working set.

There is also a multitude of visual interfaces to information providers other than digital libraries. For example, the visual search engine Grokker[1] employs Venn diagrams, as well as nested circles and squares to visualize the combined results of several web search engines. The Fed-Stats Browser [KS03] is a metadata-driven visual information browser for federal statistics that exploits folders, trees, and maps to assist the user in finding the right table, chart, or report, without being familiar with different terminologies. Mane et al. [MB06] present the SRS browser, a visual interface to about 400 biomedical databases. The application interactively displays entities and their relations, e.g. gene and protein metadata. Collages and ambient slideshows are used in [CLF+04] to enable users to gain a comprehensive view on image collections. CombinFormation [KKD+06] represents collections as compo-

---

[1] http://www.grokker.com

sitions of image and text surrogates in order to promote the understanding of individual information resources along with their relationships.

Some of the above interfaces seem to be for expert users only. For example, an average library user may find it hard to deal with scatterplots. One of the design goals for RecoDiver—the interface presented in the remainder of this chapter—is that the interface should arrange its information as clearly as possible so that it is easy to understand and to use.

To the best of knowledge, no existing interface to digital libraries has visualized the relevance between documents based on recommendations. Users would highly benefit from such an interface since recommendations often capture relevant documents that would not be found when looking for similar metadata like keywords.

Whenever there is a relation among the data elements to be visualized, the elements can be visualized as a graph. Graph drawing for information visualization has become a large research field in the past decades. The graph drawing community has presented many algorithms to layout nodes and edges of both trees and arbitrary graphs [HMM00]. Laying out a graph is certainly not trivial, e.g. determining the minimum number of edge crossings is NP-complete in general [GJ83]. However, besides graph layout, navigation and interaction in graphs is also important. Another concern lies in reducing the visual complexity of large graphs. Incremental exploration techniques provide a viable solution for both issues. At any time, the application displays only a small subgraph of the full graph. This "window" can then be moved by the user who navigates through the graph. Repositioning nodes on the screen is an important aspect. This must happen in a way by which the user can recognize nodes that have already been included in the previous window. Some research results have been published in this area. For example, Huang et al. [HEC98] present a tool to explore the WWW and Deligiannidis et al. [DSK07] use incremental exploration techniques to visualize metadata modeled using the Resource Description Framework (RDF). RecoDiver, which is introduced in the following section, pursues a similar strategy to visualize the graph of recommendations between individual documents.

9.2 RecoDiver: A Graph-Based User Interface to Recommendations

RecoDiver is described in four sections. First, the general features of the interface are depicted. Second, the mechanism for automatically

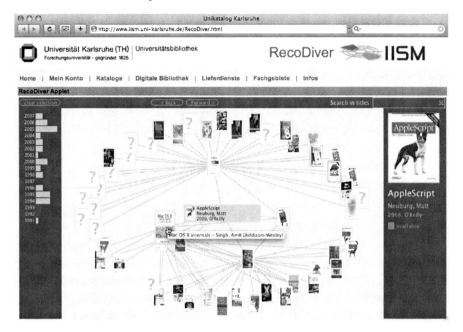

Fig. 9.1. The RecoDiver applet embedded into the website of the University Library of Karlsruhe

layouting the recommendation graph is discussed. Third, filtering tools for analyzing the documents within the graph are shown. And last, the implementation of the Java applet and the underlying software architecture is portrayed.

9.2.1 The User Interface Design of RecoDiver

The RecoDiver user interface consists of four parts (see Figure 9.1): the graph display in the center, a panel for displaying detailed information on the right, a histogram on the left, and a toolbar at the top.

The default use case of the applet is the following: the user searches the catalog, finds a document he is interested in and then switches to the RecoDiver view to find related documents. The previously viewed main document serves as a starting point for the dive into the recommendation graph. The initial view of the applet shows the main document and all first and second level recommendations. Hence, the drawn graph shows the second order neighborhood of the main document node as will be described in more detail in Section 9.2.2. For clarity reasons, the direction of the edges is not explicitly shown.

Each document node is represented by the cover image of the document. The image data is sourced from Amazon.com. Currently, a question mark is displayed, if a book cover is not available or could not be retrieved yet. In the future, it is planned to display title information instead; given the space constraints, some technical (e. g. generation of a short title) as well as design issues still need to be solved for a clear and understandable presentation. The borders of the nodes are colored to signal the availability of the document: green means the document is currently available for lending, yellow indicates that a waiting list exists, and red means that the document currently cannot be checked out at the library.

When the user moves his mouse cursor over a document node, the cover image is magnified and a tooltip with information about author, title and publisher is displayed. Clicking on a document node selects this node as the new main document, which causes the graph to update itself. The graph is completed to the second order neighborhood of the new document, while nodes farther away are cut from the displayed graph. Missing data is dynamically retrieved from the recommendation server. As soon as the structural data is complete, the new main document node is moved into the center and its recommendations are arranged accordingly.

The transition is animated to keep it easy to follow. For the animation a method by Yee et al. [YFDH01] is employed, which interpolates between polar coordinates instead of Cartesian coordinates to avoid nodes crisscrossing each other. This leads to a less confusing animation in radial layouts.

After the animated transition, the view shows the new main document and its second order neighborhood. The previous view can be restored using the history function of the applet. The history function resembles the page history of a common Internet browser application. It allows to navigate back and forth between views using the buttons located in the toolbar.

9.2.2 Radial Tree Layout

The intent was to make it as easy as possible for the user to grasp the meaning of the graph and to draw information from the visualization. The radial tree layout allows to communicate the distance of a recommended document to the main document best and aids a comprehension of "nearness".

Figure 9.2 illustrates the layout applied to the graph of recommendations. The main document is positioned in the center. The first level

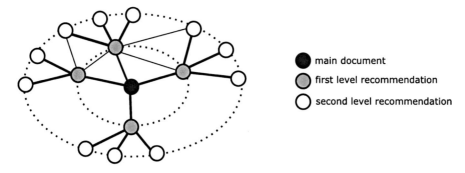

Fig. 9.2. The radial tree layout applied to a second order neighborhood of the recommendation graph

recommendations are placed on an imaginary ellipse surrounding the main document. The second level recommendations are placed on a second, bigger ellipse which encircles the first one. This property makes it easy to distinguish between first and second level recommendations.

The positions of single nodes on the ellipses are determined by a minimum spanning tree (MST), which is calculated with the main document serving as root node. The edges of the MST are emphasized in Figure 9.2 by a slightly thicker stroke.

9.2.3 Dynamic Visual Filtering

The overall clarity of the visualized graph is anti-proportional to the number of nodes. Thus, if the number of displayed documents exceeds a certain limit, the informational gain of the visualization is lost in clutter. Limiting the number of visual elements is a way to improve clarity [HMM00], but generally results in withholding information that might be useful to the user. The question was raised on how to cope with this difficulty.

The first thought was to thin out the graph by applying graph-based metrics; e. g. as used in the field of social network analysis. This approach was dropped, because it leads to fitting the recommender system to the constraints of the visualization. But the research was aimed at improving the visualization and usability of generated recommendations. Thus, a second approach was pursued which does not rely on thinning out the network of recommendations. If the amount of information cannot be reduced, the user must be provided with tools to separate the wheat from the chaff. Below, two tools are presented that allow to intuitively filter the displayed data. Both filters prove useful to restore clarity especially when the number of displayed products exceeds a certain limit.

Publication year histogram. The panel on the left side shows a histogram that visualizes the distribution of the years of publication of the currently displayed documents. This display has two purposes. The first one is simply to provide an overview to the user. The second purpose is to allow the user to filter the displayed data. When the user selects a histogram bar with his mouse, all books that were published in the selected year are highlighted, while all others are faded into the background. By holding the control key, the user can select a range or any set of years.

Filtering by publication date becomes especially useful if the user is only interested in recent publications. This is often the case, if the customer group of the information provider stems from the area of scholastic research and study. Furthermore, this tool can be used to discover trends: the histogram clearly shows an increase or decrease in published books per year.

Meta data search box. A second filter, the search box, is located in the upper right of the toolbar. It can be used to search the metadata of all displayed products. The search tool features case-insensitive incremental search. Matches are highlighted as one types to give quick feedback about the issued query. This way the user has to type less, owing to the fact that often only a few letters from a word will suffice to narrow down the selection.

When the user in Figure 9.1 on page 125 clicks on the already selected book "Mac OS X internals" by Singh, then uses the filters to restrict the selection to products that were both published in the years from 2005 to 2007 and contain the string "Tiger" in their metadata, one gets the result shown in Figure 9.3. The six highlighted recommendations can be seen to pass the filtering choices.

9.2.4 Implementation

The RecoDiver user interface is implemented in Java. Java's applet technology allows to embed the application seamlessly into the existing online catalog of the library. This is important, because RecoDiver is supposed to enhance the current OPAC as an optional research tool for (advanced) users. Another reason for choosing Java is the existence of the freely available prefuse toolkit [HCL05], a visualization framework for the Java programming language, which eases the development of graphical user interfaces due to its object-oriented framework.

Publication date selection: 2005 - 2007   Metadata search text: Tiger

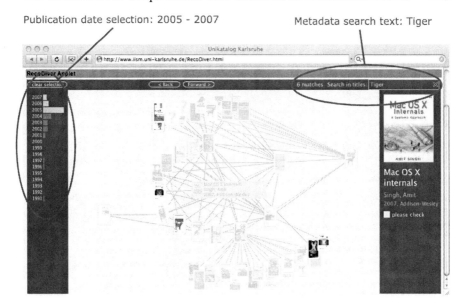

Fig. 9.3. Product filtering in RecoDiver: Publication date (2005–2007, see upper left corner) and keyword ("Tiger", see upper right corner) filtering is active

RecoDiver is powered by the distributed architecture described in Section 8.2. The system is divided into several components, each of which handles a distinct task: collecting data as well as preprocessing is done by the connection server, computing of recommendations happens on the recommendation server, and last but not least, different interface agents deliver and display the recommendations to the users. In this setting, RecoDiver is the user-interface, visualization is shifted to the user's computer.

RecoDiver retrieves recommendations by means of the same web services as the interface agent that generates the lists of recommendations in HTML (conf. Section 8.2.1). The additional features RecoDiver provides, like drawing a graph, filtering, and searching, utilize only the user's computer. Virtually no extra load is put onto the servers by the local visualization and navigation processes. However, only the number of recommendations retrieved by the RecoDiver applet are higher than that of the list-based interface since also the second level recommendations are considered and loaded. In total, however, the amount of transferred data is actually reduced, because no HTML code needs to be added; the recommendations are sent in XML-format via SOAP.

9.3 Evaluation

A usability evaluation to assess the user acceptance of RecoDiver was conducted. The questionnaire consisted of two parts. First, a subset of the questions from [Lew95] was used to evaluate the general usability of the application. The results of these general questions are presented in Section 9.3.1. The second part of the evaluation, which is discussed in Section 9.3.2, compared the existing recommendation list-based interface (see Figure 8.4 on page 96) as it is in use at the University Library of Karlsruhe with the RecoDiver interface. The survey was conducted using the open-source tool LimeSurvey[2]. The participants were 31 students and researchers of different fields from the Universität Karlsruhe (TH), most with a technical background. Due to the overall technical focus of the university and the background and spread of the evaluation group, the sample can be considered representative for the group of potential end-users of the application.

9.3.1 Usability Evaluation of RecoDiver

The usability of the RecoDiver was rated rather high. For example, about 83% of the participants were satisfied with how easy it is to use the application. 93% found the application simple to use. The percentage of users that felt comfortable using RecoDiver (71%) is a little lower. Similarly, about 10% did not find the organization of information on the screen to be clear. However, since some users were not familiar with the visualization of relational data as a graph, these results are nevertheless rather pleasant. A vast majority (93%) of the participants agreed that it was easy to learn to use RecoDiver. About 87% consented that the interface of the applet is pleasant and that they liked using it.

Only 42% agreed that RecoDiver in the current prototype state had all the functions and capabilities they expected it to have. Some suggestions were made regarding additional functionality. Most proposals longed for a better integration of the existing web services of the University Library. For example, the website of the library allows users to mark certain books as favorites, which can be accessed later on, while RecoDiver does not yet provide access to this service. Overall, 87% of the participants stated that they were satisfied with the application.

---

[2] http://www.limesurvey.org

Table 9.1. Survey results comparing RecoDiver with the list-based recommender interface

	RecoDiver	List-based interface
More intuitive	48%	35%
Better filtering	84%	10%
Connection analysis	100%	0%
Recommendation strength	26%	39%
More pleasant	77%	6%
Preferred interface	55%	19%

9.3.2 Comparative Interface Survey

The second part of the questionnaire compared the new interface with the existing list-based one. 90% of the participants stated that they are familiar with the existing recommendation service as it is in use on the website of the University Library. For the other participants this interface was demonstrated. See Section 8.3 for an evaluation of the list-based interface.

The participants were asked to compare the two interfaces. Table 9.1 presents an overview of the results. The missing percentage (to 100%) of users did not decide on the specific questions. About 48% agreed that the RecoDiver interface is more intuitive than recommendation lists; 35% stated the opposite. A vast majority (84%) attested RecoDiver to provide better filtering of recommendations. Moreover, all users found it more helpful in analyzing the connections between documents ("connection analysis" in Table 9.1). As anticipated, more users (39%) stated that recommendation lists allow to distinguish weak and strong recommendations more clearly than the RecoDiver interface ("recommendation strength"). This is due to the fact that the current RecoDiver interface does not regard the strength of a recommendation, i.e. the number of times the two documents have been purchased together, while this number is explicitly displayed on the recommendation list. When it comes to how pleasant the interfaces are, 77% found Reco-Diver more pleasant compared to 6% who voted for recommendation lists. Similarly, about 55% preferred RecoDiver over recommendation lists; only 19% chose the list interface.

The majority of the participants (about 77%) would like the University Library to provide an interface like RecoDiver by default. A slightly smaller group (74%) would even like to use a similar interface on e-commerce sites as well.

Some users stated that graphical interfaces are beneficial once their meaning has been understood. However, in some cases, especially when there were many connections between documents, the visualization was still perceived as overly complex. Nevertheless, the participants considered RecoDiver as an alternative interface that would clearly enhance the existing recommender service at the University Library or at other information providers.

9.4 Discussion and Outlook

RecoDiver is the first application for browsing recommendations of library documents on dynamic graphs. It enables the user to inspect connections between objects while providing a local view of the current neighborhood of recommendations. Visualizing the graph of recommendations without filtering is the approach presented in this chapter. This works significantly well both with smaller separated clusters of recommendations and large but not highly connected graphs. In the latter case, the background-foreground-filtering by the histogram of years of publication or the title and author search help to easily identify relevant readings for the user. As the evaluation has shown, the approach of never-filtering-out-objects comes to a limit at some point with large and highly connected graphs. These types of graphs are much more likely to appear at library applications than in e-commerce due to the difference in the magnitude of the number of products. Especially, many edges between different second level recommendations of the main document make the visual inspection complex. In these cases, the weight of the edges (the number of co-purchases of the products) can be used to thin out the graph before its presentation to the user. Minimum weight thresholds reduce the number of presented edges and documents, while minimum spanning trees can reduce the number of presented edges. A priori cluster analysis by random walks can be facilitated as well in the case of highly connected graphs (conf. Section 7.3.4). Different types of these methods were implemented in a prototype version of RecoDiver. The evaluation of different filtering algorithms showed the following: when applying one of these approaches to dynamic graphs, the main problem is the breakup into disconnected subgraphs. There is no known easy user interface for the general public (besides users trained in graph theory) to inspect such a complex process in a meaningful way at a general information provider or e-commerce site.

Considering the technical aspects of RecoDiver, various inconsistencies of the behavior of the applet with different Java versions and

web browsers were experienced. A switch from Java applet to Adobe
Flash technology seems to be a good choice to overcome this issue at
a first glance. Due to its widespread use within the WWW, the Adobe
Flash Player currently is installed on more end-users' computers than a
Java plug-in. Nevertheless, today more advanced code libraries for dynamic graph layouts exist in Java compared to Adobe Flash, easing the
development of graph-based user interfaces like RecoDiver. The flare
project[3] might make some of these libraries available in Adobe Flash
in the future. A more detailed study of the suitability of these two
programming languages together with a user survey about the tech-
nologies' user acceptance will decide about the path to take for the
final implementation of the service and its integration into the website
of an information Provider open to the general public.

---

[3] http://flare.prefuse.org

10

Discussion

Each of the previous chapters of this book has dealt with a different aspect of recommender systems for information providers. In this section, the lessons learned from each chapter are presented in condensed form and discussed. Detailed outlooks to further research on the various topics were already given in the according chapters. Please review Sections 5.5.3, 7.2.5, 8.5, and 9.4 for detailed discussions and outlooks on the presented material.

In the first chapter it was depicted that the STI market is especially suited for recommender systems due to high search costs for goods and the general problem of assessing the quality of information products. Recommender systems were defined to comprise some kind of user participation. In many e-commerce shopping sites a list of "recommendations" is given; in most cases these do not stem from user input, but from being manually placed by product managers of the shopping site according to their contribution to profit. Automatically generated recommendations which truthfully reflect the preferences of their user-community as described in this book are valuable to both providers and customers.

Chapter 2 showed that recommender systems are an important research area as they play a crucial role in the future business profile and thus in the competitive strategy of STI providers.

From Chapter 3 it can be concluded that, when one wants to start a successful recommendation service, a very strong focus should be set on the mechanism design. Currently the biggest amount of research capacity in the area of recommender systems goes into the improvement of the algorithms for the generation of recommendations, especially for collaborative filtering by means of association rules. Unfortunately, most of the developed techniques are never applied outside a laboratory prototype working with small data samples. But scalability issues can only be tested in a real service environment. Also, trustworthy feedback from a broader user community is necessary for evaluation purposes.

The overview of existing recommendation services at major information providers presented in Chapter 4 gave a somehow disappointing result. Most providers do not feature any such services yet, although some seem to work in the background and are expected to launch such services in the near future. The question remains, why are STI providers slower to act than the general business-to-consumer e-commerce? Here, three major factors can be accounted:

Missing pressure by competition. In Chapter 2 it was presented that a large part of the STI market is controlled by quasi-monopolistic publishing companies. But an institutional library can also be considered a quasi-monopolistic provider of STI to the faculty and student body of the institution. Driving to the next major city to visit the library of a different university is forbidden by the transaction cost—the access to this library might even be restricted to their faculty and student body. There are quasi-monopolistic market structures on different levels. A monopolist is not required to offer a good service if the customers depend on the good. Unfortunately, this explains, why many STI providers currently consider recommender systems as not necessary for their revenue stream or public tax funded mission. The currently ongoing change in the market structure discussed in Chapter 2 will lead to more pressure for good customer services and, thereby, to more recommender systems in the future.

Scalability issues. The number of products at STI providers, often tens of millions, forbids the application of "standard" recommendation generating algorithms. Chapter 7 presents a way out of this dilemma. The scalability is shown by the case study presented in Chapter 8.

Anonymity of users. First, the end-users of the STI (scientists etc.) are not the direct customers (i. e. for example libraries) of the publishing industry. The usage data has to be collected at providers like libraries. These public institutions in general have much higher restrictions for the protection of privacy than a single e-commerce store. Nevertheless, this work has shown that even anonymously collected usage data from libraries are sufficient (conf. Chapter 6) for setting up successful recommendation services (conf. Chapter 8).

The report on the introduction of explicit recommender systems at the University Library of Karlsruhe (conf. Chapter 5) not only shows the necessity of the correct mechanism design, but also, which other influences like the user interface play an important role when implementing recommender systems. It proves that such systems can be technically integrated as add-on services to large legacy library catalog applications. The support of different user and target groups significantly helps to channel the recommendations to appropriate recipients. To the best of knowledge, it was the first system worldwide of this kind that was actually introduced as a service to all customers at a large scientific library.

When discussing behavior-based recommender systems for STI providers, the absence of purchases—including prices and money transactions—is often stated to be a knock-out criteria for such services. The argumentation by means of revealed preferences, self-selection, and transaction costs in Chapter 6 proves this to be wrong.

Although, as mentioned before, a lot of research has been done on recommendation generating algorithms, the scalability issues due to the large number of products at STI providers as well as the cold start problem are not solved by the "traditional" algorithms. The LSD-, as well as the POSICI- and POMICI-algorithms presented in Chapter 7 are considered to hopefully bring the "traditional" methods one step further. The behavior-based recommendation service presented in Chapter 8 already relies on these methods, the development of these algorithms might be one of the reasons, why this implicit service was the first service of its kind at a large scientific library and is currently being commercialized under the BibTip brand. For the future, the item-centered approach all systems have in common makes it possible to amplify the described services by cross-usage of data. For example, the rating data can be used to further filter the behavior-based recommendations.

The general strategy of this study was the following: new scientific methods should not only be developed—and then the research finishes with a proof of concept in a laboratory prototype—but for economic research they should be tested in field experiments with real customers in services open to the general public. Although this is time-consuming, it allows for better evaluation and application forecasts. The drawback lies in many small compromises that have to be made when implementing services within websites of information providers that are service but not research oriented. Examples for these compromises have been given for the case of the user interfaces in Chapters 5 and 8. Chapter 9 depicts a user interface prototype to show, what kind of graphical interfaces the author of this book has in mind for boosting the usage of the developed recommender systems. Currently, no recommender systems exists that features such interfaces, although the user evaluation shows that it is preferred over the currently used interfaces. It is a variable that might have a significant influence on the overall usage of the recommendation services. For economical success, many variables need to be in tune.

List of Figures

List of Tables

References

Ada01.   Jean-Marc Adamo. *Data mining for association rules and sequential patterns*. Springer, New York, 2001.

AEK00.   Asim Ansari, Skander Essegaier, and Rajeev Kohli. Internet recommendation systems. *Journal of Marketing Research*, 37:363–375, August 2000.

AIS93.   Rakesh Agrawal, Tomasz Imielinski, and Arun Swami. Mining association rules between sets of items in large databases. In Peter Buneman and Sushil Jajodia, editors, *Proceedings of the ACM SIGMOD International Conference on Management of Data*, volume 22, Washington, D.C., USA, June 1993. ACM, ACM Press.

Ake70.   George A. Akerlof. The market for "lemons": Quality uncertainty and the market mechanism. *Quaterly Journal of Economics*, 84:488–500, 1970.

AL99.   Yonatan Aumann and Yehuda Lindell. A statistical theory for quantitative association rules. In U. Chaudhuri and D. Madigan, editors, *Proceedings of the 5th ACM SIGKDD international conference on Knowledge Discovey and Data Mining, San Diego, California*, pages 261–270, New York, 1999. ACM, ACM Press.

AM98.   R.L. Andrews and A.K. Manrai. Simulation experiments in choice simplifikation: The effects of task and context on forecasting performance. *Journal of Marketing Research*, 35(2):198–209, 1998.

And76.   G.E Andrews. *The Theory of Partitions*. Addison-Wesley, Reading, 1976.

Arr62.   Kenneth J. Arrow. Economic welfare and the allocation of resources for invention. In *The Rate and Direction of Inventive Activity: Economic and Social Factors*, pages 609–625. The Universities National Bureau Committee for Economic Research, Princeton University Research, Princton, 1962.

Art01.   Arthur D. Little. Zukunft der wissenschaftlichen und technischen Information in Deutschland – Ergebnisse der empirischen Untersuchungen über das Informationsverhalten von Wissenschaftlern und Unternehmen. Technical report, Arthur D. Little International, Inc., Gesellschaft für Innovationsforschung und Beratung mbH, October 2001.

ARZ99.   Christopher Avery, Paul Resnick, and Richard Zeckhauser. The market for evaluations. *American Economic Review*, 89(3):564–584, 1999.

AS94.   Rakesh Agrawal and Ramakrishnan Srikant. Fast algorithms for mining association rules. In *Proceedings of the 20th Very Large Databases Conference, Santiago, Chile*, pages 487–499, September 1994.

AS95.   R.L. Andrews and T.C. Srinivasan. Studying consideration effects in empirical choice models using scanner panel data. *Journal of Marketing Research*, 32(1):30–41, 1995.

Ask75.   Aske Research. The structure of the tooth-paste market. Technical report, Aske Research Ltd., London, 1975.

AT05.   Gediminas Adomavicius and Alexander Tuzhilin. Toward the next generation of recommender systems: a survey of the state-of-the-art and possible extensions. *IEEE Transactions on Knowledge and Data Engineering*, 17(6):734–749, June 2005.

Bas69.   Frank M. Bass. A new product growth model for consumer durables. *Management Science*, 16(5):215–227, January 1969.

BBS06.   Kirsten R. Butcher, Sonal Bhushan, and Tamara Sumner. Multimedia displays for conceptual discovery: information seeking with strand maps. *Multimedia Systems*, 11(3):236–248, 2006.

BC02.   Katy Börner and Chaomei Chen. Visual interfaces to digital libraries: Motivation, utilization, and socio-technical challenges. In Katy Börner and Chaomei Chen, editors, *Visual Interfaces to Digital Libraries*, volume 2539 of *Lecture Notes in Computer Science*, pages 1–12. Springer, 2002.

BDTD97.   A. Bechara, H. Damasio, D. Tranel, and A.R. Damasio. Deciding advantageously before knowing the advantageous strategy. *Science*, 257(28):1293–1295, 1997.

BEK+00.   D. Box, D. Ehnebuske, G. Kakivaya, A. Layman, N. Mendelsohn, H. F. Nielsen, S. Thatte, and D. Winer. *Simple Object Access Protocol (SOAP) 1.1*. World Wide Web Consortium, May 2000.

Bez81.   J. C. Bezdek. *Pattern Recognition with Fuzzy Objective Function Algorithms*. Plenum Press, NY, 1981.

BKEJ+98.   A. Brüggemann-Klein, A. Endres, E. Jessen, R. Weber, and H. Werner. Chablis – Abrechnungs- und Zahlungskonzepte für Dienstleistungen digitaler Bibliotheken. *Informatik Forschung und Entwicklung*, 13(3):169–172, 1998.

BLG00.   Kurt D. Bollacker, Steve Lawrence, and C. Lee Giles. Discovering relevant scientific literature on the web. *IEEE Intelligent Systems*, 15(2):42–47, 2000.

BLKR98.   Al Borchers, Dave Leppik, Joseph Konstan, and John Riedl. Partitioning in recommender systems. Technical Report 98-023, University of Minnesota, Minneapolis, 1998.

BMS97.   Sergey Brin, Rajeev Motwani, and Craig Silverstein. Beyond market baskets: Generalizing association rules to correlations. In Joan M. Peckman, editor, *Proceedings of the ACM SIGMOD International Conference on Management of Data, Tucson, Arizona*, volume 26, pages 265–276, New York, NY 10036, USA, May 1997. ACM Press.

Boc74.   Hans Bock. *Automatische Klassifikation*. Vandenhoeck & Ruprecht, Göttingen, 1974.

BST98.   Andreas Becks, Stefan Sklorz, and Christopher Tresp. Semantic structuring and visual querying of document abstracts in digital libraries. In Christos Nikolaou and Constantine Stephanidis, editors, *ECDL '98: Proceedings of the 2nd European Conference on Research and Advanced Technology for Digital Libraries*, volume 1513 of *Lecture Notes in Computer Science*, pages 443–458. Springer, 1998.

CCMW01.   E. Christensen, F. Curbera, G. Meredith, and S. Weerawarana. Web services description language (WSDL) 1.1. W3C note, World Wide Web Consortium, March 2001.

CE76.   P. Charlton and A. S. C. Ehrenberg. Customers of the LEP. *Applied Statistics*, 25:26–30, 1976.

CEG66.   C. Chatfield, A. S. C. Ehrenberg, and G. J. Goodhardt. Progress on a simplified model of stationary purchasing behavior. *Journal of the Royal Statistical Society A*, 129:317–367, 1966.

Chr02.   Michael G. Christel. Accessing news video libraries through dynamic information extraction, summarization, and visualization. In Katy Börner and Chaomei Chen, editors, *Visual Interfaces to Digital Libraries*, volume 2539 of *Lecture Notes in Computer Science*, pages 98–115. Springer, 2002.

Cla71.   Edward H. Clarke. Multipart pricing of public goods. *Public Choice*, 11(1):17 – 33, September 1971.

CLF⁺04.   Michelle Chang, John J. Leggett, Richard Furuta, Andruid Kerne, J. Patrick Williams, Samuel A. Burns, and Randolph G. Bias. Collection understanding. In *JCDL '04: Proceedings of the 4th ACM/IEEE-CS joint conference on Digital libraries*, pages 334–342, New York, NY, USA, 2004. ACM Press.

Coa37.   Ronald H. Coase. The nature of the firm. *Economica*, 4(16):386–405, November 1937.

Dea97.   R. Dearing et al. Higher education in the learning society. The report of the national committee of inquiry into higher education (NCIHE), 1997. http://www.leeds.ac.uk/educol/ncihe/.

Deu01.   Deutscher Bibliotheksverband. Stellungnahme des Deutschen Biliotheksverbands zum Strategiekonzept "Zukunft der wissenschaftlichen und technischen Information", July 2001.   http://www.bibliotheksverband.de/dbv/aktuelles/ adl4-Geisselmann-30-7-011.pdf.

DGL+06.   Mathias Dewatripont, Victor Ginsburgh, Patrick Legros, Alexis Walckiers, Jean-Pierre Devroey, Marianne Dujardin, Françoise Vandooren, Pierre Dubois, Jérôme Foncel, Marc Ivaldi, and Marie-Dominique Heusse. Study on the economic and technical evolution of the scientific publication markets in europe. Technical report, European Commission, Belgium, January 2006.

DHS01.   Richard O. Duda, Peter E. Hart, and David G. Stork. *Pattern Classification*. Wiley-Interscience, NY, 2. edition, 2001.

DSK+05.   M. Deppe, W. Schwindt, H. Kugel, H. Plassmann, and P. Kenning. Nonlinear response within the medial prefrontal cortex reveal when specific implicit information influences economic decision making. *Journal of Neuroimaging*, 15(2):171–182, 2005.

DSK07.   Leon Deligiannidis, Amit Sheth, and Krys Kochut. User-centered incremental RDF data exploration and visualization. In *ESWC 2007: Proceedings of the 4th European Semantic Web Conference*, 2007.

Dus04.   Naomi Dushay. Visualizing bibliographic metadata – a virtual (book) spine viewer. *D-Lib Magazine*, 10(10), October 2004.

EA96.   European Commission, DG XIII/E and Andersen Consulting. Strategic developments for the European publishing industry towards the year 2000: Europe's multimedia challenge. Technical report, European Commission, 1996.

Ehr88.   A. S. C. Ehrenberg. *Repeat-Buying: Facts, Theory and Applications*. Charles Griffin & Company Ltd, London, 2. edition, 1988.

Emo97.   Winand Emons. Credence goods and fraudulent experts. *RAND Journal of Economic*, 28(1):107–120, 1997.

Fel71.   William Feller. *An Introduction to Probability Theory and Its Application*, volume 2. John Wiley, New York, 2 edition, 1971.

FFW91.   Richard H. Fowler, Wendy A. L. Fowler, and Bradley A. Wilson. Integrating query, thesaurus, and documents through a common visual representation. In *Proceedings of the 14th Annual International ACM SIGIR Conference on Research and Development in Information Retrieval*, pages 142–151, Chicago, Illinois, USA, October 1991. ACM Press.

FGSN06.   Markus Franke, Andreas Geyer-Schulz, and Andreas Neumann. Building recommendations from random walks on library OPAC usage data. In Sergio Zani, Andrea Cerioli, Marco Riani, and Maurizio Vichi, editors, *Data Analysis, Classification and the Forward Search*, Studies in Classification, Data Analysis, and Knowledge Organization, pages 235–246, Berlin Heidelberg New York, 2006. Classification and Data Analysis Group (CLADAG) of the Italian Statistical Society, Springer.

FGSN08.   Markus Franke, Andreas Geyer-Schulz, and Andreas W. Neumann. Recommender services in scientific digital libraries. In George A. Tsihrintzis and Lakhmi C. Jain, editors, *Multimedia Services in Intelligent Environments*, Studies in Computational Intelligence, pages 377–417. Springer, Berlin / Heidelberg, 2008.

FHN+93.   Edward A. Fox, Deborah Hix, Lucy T. Nowell, Dennis J. Brueni, William C. Wake, Lenwood S. Heath, and Durgesh Rao. Users, user interfaces, and objects: Envision, a digital library. *Journal of the American Society for Information Science*, 44(8):480–491, 1993.

FR98.   George W. Furnas and Samuel J. Rauch. Considerations for information environments and the navique workspace. In *DL '98: Proceedings of the third ACM conference on Digital Libraries*, pages 79–88, New York, NY, USA, 1998. ACM Press.

FT95.   Drew Fudenberg and Jean Tirole. *Game Theory*. MIT Press, 1995.

GBL98.   C. Lee Giles, Kurt Bollacker, and Steve Lawrence. CiteSeer: An automatic citation indexing system. In Ian Witten, Rob Akscyn, and Frank M. Shipman III, editors, *Digital Libraries 98 - The Third ACM Conference on Digital Libraries*, pages 89–98, Pittsburgh, PA, June 23–26 1998. ACM Press.

GGJ+05.   Christian Grün, Jens Gerken, Hans-Christian Jetter, Werner König, and Harald Reiterer. MedioVis – A user-centred library metadata browser. In Andreas Rauber, Stavros Christodoulakis, and A. Min Tjoa, editors, *ECDL 2005: Proceedings of the 9th European Conference on Research and Advanced Technology for Digital Libraries*, volume 3652 of *Lecture Notes in Computer Science*, pages 174–185. Springer, 2005.

GGSHST02.   Wolfgang Gaul, Andreas Geyer-Schulz, Michael Hahsler, and Lars Schmidt-Thieme. eMarketing mittels Recommendersystemen. *Marketing – Zeitschrift für Forschung und Praxis (ZFP)*, 24:47–55, 2002.

GJ83.   M. R. Garey and D. S. Johnson. Crossing number is NP-complete. *SIAM Journal on Algebraic and Discrete Methods*, 4(3):312–316, 1983.

GNOT92.   David Goldberg, David Nichols, Brian Oki, and Douglas Terry. Using collaborative filtering to weave an information tapestry. *Communications of the ACM*, 35(12):61–70, December 1992.

GPJB05.   Lance Good, Ashok C. Popat, William C. Janssen, and Eric
            Bier. A fluid treemap interface for personal digital libraries. In
            *JCDL '05: Proceedings of the 5th ACM/IEEE-CS joint confer-
            ence on Digital libraries*, pages 408–408, New York, NY, USA,
            2005. ACM Press.

Gre05.   Gerry Grenier. Path to document recommendation services:
            Technologies that enabled the development of on-line informa-
            tion systems. Presentation held at the ACS National Meeting
            #230, 2005.

Gro73.   Theodore Groves. Incentives in teams. *Econometrica*, 41(4):617
            – 631, July 1973.

Grö05.   Christian Grönroos. *Service management and marketing*. Wiley,
            Chichester, England, 2. ed., repr. edition, 2005.

GSH02.   Andreas Geyer-Schulz and Michael Hahsler. Evaluation of rec-
            ommender algorithms for an internet information broker based
            on simple association-rules and on repeat-buying theory. In
            Proceedings of the WebKDD, Edmonton, Alberta, Canada, July
            2002. ACM, ACM Press.

GSHJ01.   Andreas Geyer-Schulz, Michael Hahsler, and Maximillian Jahn.
            Educational and scientific recommender systems: Designing the
            information channels of the virtual university. *International
            Journal of Engineering Education*, 17(2):153–163, 2001.

GSHJ02.   Andreas Geyer-Schulz, Michael Hahsler, and Maximilian Jahn.
            A customer purchase incidence model applied to recommender
            services. In R. Kohavi et al., editor, *Proceedings of the WebKDD
            – Mining log data across all customer touchpoints*, volume 2356
            of *Lecture Notes in Artificial Intelligence LNAI*, pages 25–47,
            Berlin, 2002. ACM, Springer-Verlag.

GSHNT03a.   Andreas Geyer-Schulz, Michael Hahlser, Andreas Neumann, and
            Anke Thede. Recommenderdienste für wissenschaftliche Biblio-
            theken und Bibliotheksverbünde. In Andreas Geyer-Schulz and
            Alfred Taudes, editors, *Informationswirtschaft – ein Sektor mit
            Zukunft*, volume P-33 of *GI-Edition – Lecture Notes in Infor-
            matics (LNI)*, Bonn, 2003. Köllen.

GSHNT03b.   Andreas Geyer-Schulz, Michael Hahsler, Andreas Neumann, and
            Anke Thede. Behavior-based recommender systems as value-
            added services for scientific libraries. In Hamparsum Bozdogan,
            editor, *Statistical Data Mining & Knowledge Discovery*. Chap-
            man & Hall / CRC, 2003.

GSHNT03c.   Andreas Geyer-Schulz, Michael Hahsler, Andreas Neumann, and
            Anke Thede. An integration strategy for distributed recom-
            mender services in legacy library systems. In Martin Schader,
            Wolfgang Gaul, and Maurizio Vichi, editors, *Between Data Sci-
            ence And Applied Data Analysis*, Studies in Classification, Data

Analysis, and Knowledge Organization, Heidelberg-Berlin, 2003. Springer.

GSHT03.   Andreas Geyer-Schulz, Michael Hahsler, and Anke Thede. Comparing association-rules and repeat-buying based recommender systems in a b2b environment. In Martin Schader, Wolfgang Gaul, and Maurizio Vichi, editors, *Between Data Science And Applied Data Analysis*, Studies in Classification, Data Analysis, and Knowledge Organization, Heidelberg-Berlin, 2003. Springer.

GSNHS03. Andreas Geyer-Schulz, Andreas Neumann, Annika Heitmann, and Karsten Stroborn. Strategic positioning options for scientific libraries in markets of scientific and technical information – the economic impact of digitization. *Journal of Digital Information*, 4(2), 2003.

GSNT03a. Andreas Geyer-Schulz, Andreas Neumann, and Anke Thede. An architecture for behavior-based library recommender systems. *Information Technology and Libraries*, 22(4):165–174, December 2003.

GSNT03b. Andreas Geyer-Schulz, Andreas Neumann, and Anke Thede. Others also use: A robust recommender system for scientific libraries. In Traugott Koch and Ingeborg Torvik Sølvberg, editors, *Research and Advanced Technology for Digital Libraries*, volume 2769 of *Lecture Notes in Computer Science*, pages 113–125, Berlin Heidelberg New York, 2003. Springer.

HCL05.   Jeffrey Heer, Stuart K. Card, and James A. Landay. prefuse: a toolkit for interactive information visualization. In Gerrit C. van der Veer and Carolyn Gale, editors, *Proceedings of ACM CHI 2005 Conference on Human Factors in Computing Systems*, volume 1 of *Interactive information visualization*, pages 421–430. ACM, 2005.

Hec79.   James J. Heckman. Sample selection bias as a specification error. *Econometrica*, 47(1):153–161, January 1979.

HEC98.   Mao Lin Huang, Peter Eades, and Robert F. Cohen. WebOFDAV – navigating and visualizing the web on-line with animated context swapping. In *WWW7: Proceedings of the seventh international conference on World Wide Web 7*, pages 638–642, Amsterdam, The Netherlands, 1998. Elsevier Science Publishers B. V.

HJSS06.   Andreas Hotho, Robert Jäschke, Christoph Schmitz, and Gerd Stumme. BibSonomy: A social bookmark and publication sharing system. In Aldo de Moor, Simon Polovina, and Harry Delugach, editors, *Proceedings of the First Conceptual Structures Tool Interoperability Workshop at the 14th International Conference on Conceptual Structures*, pages 87–102, Aalborg, 2006. Aalborg Universitetsforlag.

HKTR04.   Jonathan L. Herlocker, Joseph A. Konstan, Loren G. Terveen, and John T. Riedl. Evaluating collaborative filtering recommender systems. *ACM Transactions on Informations Systems*, 22(1):5–53, January 2004.

HKW94.   Matthias Hemmje, Clemens Kunkel, and Alexander Willett. Lyberworld – a visualization user interface supporting fulltext retrieval. In *SIGIR '94: Proceedings of the 17th annual international ACM SIGIR conference on Research and Development in Information Retrieval*, pages 249–259, New York, NY, USA, 1994. Springer-Verlag New York, Inc.

HMM00.   Ivan Herman, Guy Melançon, and M. Scott Marshall. Graph visualization and navigation in information visualization: a survey. *IEEE Transactions on Visualization and Computer Graphics*, 6(1):24–43, 2000.

HS85.   James J. Heckman and Guilherme Sedlacek. Heterogeneity, aggregation, and market wage functions: An empirical model of self-selection in the labor market. *The Journal of Political Economy*, 93(6):1077–1125, December 1985.

HS90.   James J. Heckman and Guilherme L. Sedlacek. Self-selection and the distribution of hourly wages. *Journal of Labor Economics*, 8(1):S329–S363., January 1990.

JKB97.   Norman L. Johnson, Samuel Kotz, and N. Balakrishnan. *Discrete Multivariate Distributions*. John Wiley, New York, 1997.

JKK93.   Norman L. Johnson, Adrienne W. Kemp, and Samuel Kotz. *Univariate Discrete Distributions*. Wiley Series in Probability and Mathematical Statistics. John Wiley, 2. edition, 1993.

Jon98.   Steve Jones. Graphical query specification and dynamic result previews for a digital library. In *UIST '98: Proceedings of the 11th annual ACM symposium on User interface software and technology*, pages 143–151, New York, NY, USA, 1998. ACM Press.

Kau05.   Kaufman-Wills Group, LLC. The facts about open access – a study of the financial and non-financial effects of alternative business models for scholarly journals. Technical report, Association of Learned and Professional Society Publishers, Worthing, West Sussex, UK, 2005.

KGKF01.   Rüdiger Klatt, Konstantin Gavriilidis, Kirsten Kleinsimlinghaus, and Maresa Feldmann. Nutzung und Potenziale der innovativen Mediennutzung im Lernalltag der Hochschulen, 2001. BMBF-Studie, http://www.stefi.de/.

Kie01.   Kienbaum Management Consultants. Geschäftsmodelle für elektronische Informationsangebote zwischen Verlagen und Bibliotheken. Technical report, BMBF, July 2001.

KKD+06.   Andruid Kerne, Eunyee Koh, Blake Dworaczyk, J. Michael Mistrot, Hyun Choi, Steven M. Smith, Ross Graeber, Daniel Caruso,

Andrew Webb, Rodney Hill, and Joel Albea. combinFormation: a mixed-initiative system for representing collections as compositions of image and text surrogates. In *JCDL '06: Proceedings of the 6th ACM/IEEE-CS joint conference on Digital libraries*, pages 11–20, New York, NY, USA, 2006. ACM Press.

KMM+97. Joseph Konstan, Bradley Miller, David Maltz, Jonathan Herlocker, Lee Gordon, and John Riedl. Grouplens: Applying Collaborative Filtering to Usernet News. *Communications of the ACM*, 40(3):77–87, March 1997.

Kot80. Philip Kotler. *Marketing management: analysis, planning, and control.* Prentice-Hall, Englewood Cliffs, 4. edition, 1980.

KP02. Alexis H. Kunz and Dieter Pfaff. Agency theory, performance evaluation, and the hypothetical construct of intrinsic motivation. *Accounting, Organizations and Society*, 27(3):275–295, 2002.

KRML03. Peter Klein, Harald Reiterer, Frank Müller, and Tobias Limbach. Metadata visualisation with vismeB. In Ebad Banissi, Katy Börner, Chaomei Chen, Gordon Clapworthy, Carsten Maple, Amy Lobben, Christopher J. Moore, Jonathan C. Roberts, Anna Ursyn, and Jian Zhang, editors, *IV 2003: Proceedings of the Seventh International Conference on Information Visualization*, pages 600–605. IEEE Computer Society, 2003.

KS02. Karl-Heinz Ketterer and Karsten Stroborn, editors. *Handbuch ePayment.* Deutscher Wirtschaftsdienst, Köln, 2002.

KS03. Bill Kules and Ben Shneiderman. Designing a metadata-driven visual information browser for federal statistics. In *dg.o '03: Proceedings of the 2003 annual national conference on Digital government research*, pages 1–6. Digital Government Research Center, 2003.

Lew95. James R. Lewis. IBM computer usability satisfaction questionnaires: Psychometric evaluation and instructions for use. *International Journal of Human-Computer Interaction*, 7(1):57–78, 1995.

LGB99. Steve Lawrence, C. Lee Giles, and Kurt D. Bollacker. Digital libraries and autonomous citation indexing. *IEEE Computer*, 32(6):67–71, 1999.

LJB01. Gregory D Linden, Jannifer A. Jacobi, and Eric A. Benson. Collaborative recommendations using item-to-item similarity mappings. U.S. Patent 157198, assignee amazon.com, 2001.

LN98. Sauli Laitinen and Anssi Neuvonen. BALTICSEAWEB - geographic user interface to bibliographic information. In Christos Nikolaou and Constantine Stephanidis, editors, *ECDL '98: Proceedings of the 2nd European Conference on Research and Advanced Technology for Digital Libraries*, volume 1513 of *Lecture Notes in Computer Science*, pages 651–652. Springer, 1998.

LR04.   Shyong K. Lam and John Riedl. Shilling recommender systems
             for fun and profit. In *WWW '04: Proceedings of the 13th inter-
             national conference on World Wide Web*, pages 393–402, New
             York, NY, USA, 2004. ACM Press.
LSY03.   Greg Linden, Brent Smith, and Jeremy York. Amazon.com rec-
             ommendations: Item-to-item collaborative filtering. *IEEE In-
             ternet Computing*, 7(1):76–80, 2003.
MAC+02.   Sean M. McNee, Istvan Albert, Dan Cosley, Prateep Gopalkrish-
             nan, Shyong K. Lam, Al Mamunur Rashid, Joseph A. Konstan,
             and John Riedl. On the recommending of citations for research
             papers. In *CSCW '02: Proceedings of the 2002 ACM conference
             on Computer supported cooperative work*, pages 116–125, New
             York, 2002. ACM Press.
Mad01.   G.S. Maddala. *Introduction to Econometrics*. John Wiley,
             Chichester, 2001.
MB06.   Ketan K. Mane and Katy Börner. SRS Browser: A visual in-
             terface to the sequence retrieval system. In *Visualization and
             Data Analysis*, volume 6060 of *Proceedings of SPIE*, pages 1–11,
             January 2006.
MHML05.   Linn Marks, Jeremy A. T. Hussell, Tamara M. McMahon, and
             Richard Luce. ActiveGraph: A digital library visualization tool.
             International Journal on Digital Libraries, 5(1):57–69, March
             2005.
MN02.   Andreas Mild and Martin Natter. Collaborative filtering or re-
             gression models for internet recommendation systems? *Jour-
             nal of Targeting, Measurement and Analysis for Marketing*,
             10(4):304 – 313, January 2002.
MR92.   Paul Milgrom and John Roberts. *Economics, Organization and
             Management*. Prentice-Hall, Upper Saddle River, 1992.
Neu07a.   Andreas W. Neumann. Motivating and supporting user inter-
             action with recommender systems. In László Kovács, Norbert
             Fuhr, and Carlo Meghini, editors, *Research and Advanced Tech-
             nology for Digital Libraries*, LNCS 4675, pages 428–439, Berlin
             Heidelberg New York, 2007. Springer.
Neu07b.   Andreas W. Neumann. Price elasticity of digital scientific infor-
             mation – a field experiment. *IADIS International Journal on
             WWW/Internet*, 5(2):1–11, December 2007.
Neu07c.   Andreas W. Neumann. Pricing of digital scientific information.
             In Piet Kommers, editor, *Proceedings of the IADIS International
             Conference e-Society 2007*, pages 105–112. IADIS Press, 2007.
NFH+96.   Lucy T. Nowell, Robert K. France, Deborah Hix, Lenwood S.
             Heath, and Edward A. Fox. Visualizing search results: Some
             alternatives to query-document similarity. In Hans-Peter Frei,
             Donna Harman, Peter Schäuble, and Ross Wilkinson, editors,
             SIGIR '96: Proceedings of the 19th Annual International ACM

SIGIR Conference on Research and Development in Information Retrieval, pages 67–75. ACM Press, 1996.

NGS08.   Andreas W. Neumann and Andreas Geyer-Schulz. Applying small sample test statistics for behavior-based recommendations. In Christine Preisach, Hans Burkhardt, Lars Schmidt-Thieme, and Reinhold Decker, editors, *Data Analysis, Machine Learning, and Applications*, pages 541–549, Berlin Heidelberg, 2008. Springer.

NHS02.   Andreas Neumann, Annika Heitmann, and Karsten Stroborn. Auswirkungen der Digitalisierung auf Fachinformationsmärkte am Beispiel kostenpflichtiger Dienste hybrider Bibliotheken. In Klaus P. Jantke, Wolfgang S. Wittig, and Joerg Herrmann, editors, *Von e-Learning bis e-Payment: Das Internet als sicherer Marktplatz*, infix, pages 365–376, Berlin, 2002. Akademischen Verlagsgesellschaft.

NM75.   Chem L. Narayana and Ram J. Markin. Consumer behavior and product performance: An alternative conceptualization. *Journal of Marketing*, 39(4):1–6, October 1975.

NPR08.   Andreas W. Neumann, Marc Philipp, and Felix Riedel. Reco-Diver: Browsing behavior-based recommendations on dynamic graphs. *AI Communications*, 2008. To appear.

OMS05.   Albert Over, Friedhelm Maiworm, and André Schelewsky. *Publikationsstrategien im Wandel?* Wiley-VCH, Weinheim, Germany, 2005.

PBMW98.   Lawrence Page, Sergy Brin, Rajeev Motwani, and Terry Winograd. The page rank citation ranking: Bringing order to the web. Technical Report 0, Computer Science Department, Stanford University, January 1998.

PI93.   B. Joseph Pine II. *Mass Customization.* Harvard Business School Press, Boston, Massachusetts, 1993.

PIPR95.   B. Joseph Pine II, D. Peppers, and M. Rogers. Do you want to keep your customers forever? *Harvard Business School Review*, 5:105–111, 1995.

Por80.   Martin F. Porter. An algorithm for suffix stripping. *Program*, 14:130–137, 1980.

Pre99.   Canice Prendergast. The provision of incentives in firms. *Journal of Economic Literature*, 37(1):7–64, 1999.

Pri62.   I. Prigogine. *Non-equilibrium statistical Mechanics*. John Wiley & Sons, New York, 1962.

PW78.   N. Powell and J. Westwood. Buyer-behaviour in management education. *Applied Statistics*, 27:69–72, 1978.

RB99.   Andreas Rauber and Harald Bina. A metaphor graphics based representation of digital libraries on the world wide web: Using the libViewer to make metadata visible. In *DEXA '99: Proceedings of the 10th International Workshop on Database and Expert Systems Applications*, LNCS, pages 286–290, 1999.

RIBR94.   Paul Resnick, Neophytos Iacovou, Peter Bergstrom, and John Riedl. GroupLens: An open architecture for collaborative filtering of netnews. In *Proceedings of the conference on computer supported cooperative work*, pages 175–186. ACM Press, 1994.

ROW01.   Ulrich Riehm, Carsten Orwat, and Bernd Wingert. Online-Buchhandel in Deutschland – Die Buchhandelsbranche vor der Herausforderung des Internet. Technical Report 192, Institut für Technikfolgenabschätzung und Systemanalyse, Forschungszentrum Karlsruhe, June 2001.

RS76.   Michael Rothschild and Joseph Stiglitz. Equilibrium in competitive insurance markets: An essay on the economics of imperfect information. *Quarterly Journal of Economics*, 80:629–649, 1976.

RV97.   Paul Resnick and Hal R. Varian. Recommender systems. *Communications of the ACM*, 40(9):56–58, March 1997.

Sam38a.   Paul A. Samuelson. A note on the pure theory of consumer's behaviour. *Economica*, 5(17):61 – 71, 1938.

Sam38b.   Paul A. Samuelson. A note on the pure theory of consumer's behaviour: An addendum. *Economica*, 5(19):353–354, 1938.

Sam48.   Paul A. Samuelson. Consumption theory in terms of revealed preference. *Economica*, 15(60):243–253, 1948.

SBAG03.   Tamara Sumner, Sonal Bhushan, Faisal Ahmad, and Qianyi Gu. Designing a language for creating conceptual browsing interfaces for digital libraries. In *JCDL'03: Proceedings of the 3rd ACM/IEEE-CS Joint Conference on Digital Libraries*, Designing and accessing scientific digital libraries, pages 258–260, 2003.

SCL+99.   Marc M. Sebrechts, John V. Cugini, Sharon J. Laskowski, Joanna Vasilakis, and Michael S. Miller. Visualization of search results: a comparative evaluation of text, 2D, and 3D interfaces. In *SIGIR '99: Proceedings of the 22nd annual international ACM SIGIR conference on Research and development in information retrieval*, pages 3–10, New York, NY, USA, 1999. ACM Press.

Shi07.   Ali Shiri. The use of metadata in visual interfaces to digital libraries. In László Kovács, Norbert Fuhr, and Carlo Meghini, editors, *Research and Advanced Technology for Digital Libraries*, LNCS 4675, pages 489–494, Berlin Heidelberg, 2007. Springer.

Sic82.   H. S. Sichel. Repeat-buying and a Poisson-generalised inverse Gaussian distributions. *Applied Statistics*, 31:193–204, 1982.

Sim71.   Herbert A. Simon. Designing organisations for an information-rich world. In Martin Greenberger, editor, *Computers, Communications, and the Public Interest*, pages 40–41. The Johns Hopkins Press, 1971.

SKCvS01.   T. R. Schatzki, K. Knorr Cetina, and E. von Savigny. *The practice turn in contemporary theory.* Routledge, New York, 2001.

SKKR02.   Badrul M. Sarwar, George Karypis, Joseph Konstan, and John Riedl. Recommender systems for large-scale e-commerce: Scalable neighborhood formation using clustering. In *Proceedings of the Fifth International Conference on Computer and Information Technology*, Bangladesh, 2002.

SKR99.   J. Ben Schafer, Joseph A. Konstan, and John Riedl. Recommender system in e-commerce. In *Proceedings of the ACM Conference on Electronic Commerce*, pages 115–152. ACM, 1999.

SKR01.   J. Ben Schafer, Joseph A. Konstan, and John Riedl. E-commerce recommendation applications. *Data Mining and Knowledge Discovery*, 5:115–152, 2001.

Spe74.   Michael A. Spence. *Market Signaling: Information Transfer in Hiring and Related Screening Processes.* Harvard University Press, Cambridge, Massachusetts, 1974.

S.R65.   S.R.S. The S.R.S. motorists panel. Technical report, Sales Research Service, London, 1965.

SS87.   Susan Spiggle and Murphy A. Sewall. A choice sets model of retail selection. *Journal of Marketing*, 51:97–111, April 1987.

SS97.   Christoph Schlueter and Michael J. Shaw. A strategic framework for developing electronic commerce. *IEEE Internet Computing*, 1(6):20–28, November 1997.

SSP03.   Joachim Schöll and Elisabeth Schöll-Paschinger. Classification by restricted random walks. *Patt. Recogn.*, 36(6):1279–1290, 2003.

Sti61.   George J. Stigler. The economics of information. *The Journal of Political Economy*, 69(3):213–225, June 1961.

SV99.   Carl Shapiro and Hal R. Varian. *Information rules.* Harvard Business School, 1999.

SY73.   Gerard Salton and C.S. Yang. On the specification of term values in automatic indexing. *Journal of Documentation*, 29:351–372, 1973.

TMA+04.   Roberto Torres, Sean M. McNee, Mara Abel, Joseph A. Konstan, and John Riedl. Enhancing digital libraries with techlens+. In *JCDL '04: Proceedings of the 4th ACM/IEEE-CS joint conference on Digital libraries*, pages 228–236, New York, 2004. ACM Press.

Tof70.   Alvin Toffler. *Future Shock.* Random House, New York, 1970.

UF98.   Lyle H. Ungar and Dean P. Foster. Clustering methods for collaborative filtering. In *Proc. Workshop on Recommendation Systems*, Menlo Park, 1998. AAAI Press.

Whi01.   John White. ACM opens portal. *Communications of the ACM*, 44(7):14–16, 2001.

WS06.   Colleen Whitney and Lisa Schiff. The Melvyl recommender
            project: Developing library recommendation services. *D-Lib
            Magazine*, 12(12), December 2006.
WT87.   Udo Wagner and Alfred Taudes. Stochastic models of consumer
            behaviour. *European Journal of Operational Research*, 29(1):1–
            23, 1987.
YFDH01.   Ka-Ping Yee, D. Fisher, R. Dhamija, and M. Hearst. Animated
            exploration of dynamic graphs with radial layout. In *InfoVis
            2001: IEEE Symposium on Information Visualization*, pages 43–
            50, Washington, Brussels, Tokyo, October 2001. IEEE.
Yia97.   Peter Yianilos. The LikeIt intelligent string comparison facility.
            Technical Report 97-093, NEC Research Institute, 1997.

Printed in the United States
143406LV00001BB/3/P